The Readymade Family:
How to Be a Stepparent
and Survive

Books by André Bustanoby—

But I Didn't Want a Divorce
*Just Talk to Me: Talking and Listening for a Happier
    Marriage* (with Fay Bustanoby)
*The Readymade Family: How to Be a Stepparent and
    Survive*

The Readymade Family

How to Be a Stepparent and Survive

André Bustanoby

ZONDERVAN
PUBLISHING HOUSE
OF THE ZONDERVAN CORPORATION | GRAND RAPIDS, MICHIGAN 49506

Edited by Linda DeVries
Designed by Ann Cherryman

Scripture quotations are from *The Holy Bible: The New International Version,* copyright © 1978 by the New York International Bible Society.

On occasion, the pronoun *he* is used generically and should be understood to refer to both male and female.

Library of Congress Cataloging in Publication Data

Bustanoby, André.
  The readymade family.

  Includes bibliographical references and index.
  1. Stepparents—United States. 2. Parenting—United States. 3. Stepparents—United States—Family relationships. 4. Stepchildren—United States—Family relationships. I. Title.
HQ759.92.B87 1982   646.7'8   82-16099
ISBN 0-310-45361-5

Printed in the United States of America

82 83 84 85 86 87 88 — 10 9 8 7 6 5 4 3 2

Contents

Preface

Every year nearly one million children in the United States under the age of eighteen will see a parent remarry. Well over half a million adults will become stepparents.[1] If the present trend toward divorce and remarriage continues, by 1990 stepfamilies will outnumber biological families.

This development has generated a spate of books on stepparenting, so why another book? Almost every book on stepparenting opens with the caution that the stepfamily is different from the nonstepfamily or "natural" family. Therefore, it is maintained, we cannot expect stepfamilies to function as natural families. In many respects this is true, and I make these differences clear in this book. But as I read the books on the market, I get a bit uneasy because it seems to me that some basic rules of husband/wife and parent/child relationships are ignored in the name of differentness. Let me give two examples.

First, the husband/wife relationship should be the primary relationship, whether in the natural family or the stepfamily. The children will grow up, leave home, and make lives for themselves. But ideally, the husband and wife will remain together for the rest of their lives. Too often, however, the biological parent in the stepfamily will establish a stronger, more enduring alliance with the children than with the new spouse, the stepparent. More often than not this is done out of guilt. As one mother said to me,

"I have deprived my children of their father. I can't let them feel that they're losing their mother too."

Second, biological parents in many stepfamilies often do not practice the principles of good parenting (again, most often out of guilt) because they have been told that the stepfamily is different. In the name of differentness they look for new parenting rules.

A father told me, "I know my daughters get away with murder. But we just can't come down hard on them. They've had enough trouble with the divorce and adjusting to their stepmother. You know that a stepmother can't take the place of a mother."

It is true that a stepmother doesn't *replace* a mother. But neither does a teacher in a classroom replace mother when a child goes to school. The child is expected to behave and treat the teacher with respect, even though the teacher is not mother. Likewise, a stepmother, though she is not a replacement for mother, is the female adult leader in the custodial family and is to be accorded the respect due her position.

Though I understand the differentness that exists in stepfamilies, the emphasis of this book will be on the principles of good parenting and how to avoid letting those principles be eroded by the excuse "Stepfamilies are different." The principles of good parenting and good interpersonal relations apply to both natural families and stepfamilies.

1.

Stepfamilies
Are Different

Both Frank and Nancy have been married before. Nancy has two daughters, eight and nine, from her first marriage. Frank has a son and a daughter from his first marriage. His daughter is fifteen and his son, Eddie, is sixteen.

When Frank married Nancy, his son, Eddie, stayed with his mother to finish high school while Frank moved to another city to take a new job and make a home with Nancy, her two daughters, and his own daughter.

This new family arrangement made Nancy the custodial mother of her two daughters, the custodial stepmother of Frank's daughter, and the noncustodial stepmother of Frank's son. It made Frank the custodial father of his daughter, the custodial stepfather of Nancy's two daughters, and the noncustodial father of his son.

Because of visitation rights the family is not static. Occasionally Frank's son comes to visit him and Nancy, particularly on holidays and vacations. His daughter goes away to see her mother.

Nancy's daughters are on the move also. They go to visit their father every other weekend.

Now add to this scenario three more people. Frank's former wife remarries, and her mother comes to live with her, her new husband, and her son, Eddie. Nancy's former husband remarries.

This means that Eddie is faced with a growing cast of authority figures. He has a custodial mother, a custodial stepfather, a live-in grandmother, a noncustodial father, and a noncustodial stepmother. In addition to these direct influences on his life, Eddie faces some indirect influence from his stepmother's former husband. Add to Eddie's difficulties the fact that Nancy hates to have Eddie visit. She thinks Eddie is crude and a bad influence on the girls. Nancy's former husband gloats over this and uses it to fan the flames of discontent. "Eddie's just like his father— crude," says Nancy's former husband. His new wife chimes in, "I don't see how Nancy could have given up my wonderful man for a person like Frank."

There are three adult men and four adult women making an impact on Eddie's life and doing so in a destructive way. The men are his father, his stepfather, and his stepmother's former husband. The women are his mother, his maternal grandmother, his stepmother, and his stepmother's former husband's wife!

Does this cast of characters boggle your mind? Is it hard to follow? Think of poor Eddie! On page 11, I visualize the cast of characters and the direct and indirect relationships among them. Eddie is singled out only as an example of how difficult it is to be caught up in such a complex system. The others in the system also struggle.

What the Experts Are Saying

More than 40 percent of second marriages end in divorce within the first five years of marriage. Where there are children, the family breaks up too. Why so many broken families? One would think that the lessons learned in the first marriages will make the second marriages stronger. Not so, say the experts.

Stepfamilies face pressures absent in the natural family. Ruth Roosevelt and Jeannette Lofas, both stepmothers themselves, write, "The most pervasive myth in a stepmarriage is that the family should function as does a natural family. It doesn't. Classic mistake number one is to think that it will. It can't."[1]

Why is it that stepfamilies can't function as natural families? Two reasons are offered: the cast of characters involved in the

THE CAST OF CHARACTERS
and Their Influence on Each Other in a Sample Stepfamily

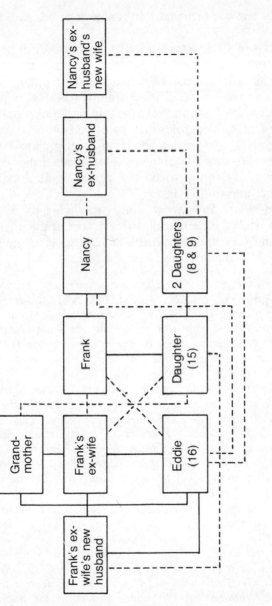

—————— Solid line represents direct influence through living in the same house.

- - - - - - Broken line represents indirect influence, as through visitation of the child in the noncustodial parent's home.

stepfamily and the fact that they came together as a readymade family.

The Cast of Characters. Family therapist Virginia Satir says that the "blended family" (stepfamily) is made up by and interwoven with a large cast of characters that either supports or detracts from the system. The stepfamily has less control over its destiny because of the interrelationship of the many adults in the family system. Critical roles may be played by the absent parents, former spouses, and an extended family of grandparents, aunts, and uncles. We saw this in the case of Eddie at the beginning of this chapter. By trying to be the typical natural family, stepfamilies get into trouble fast.[2]

The newsletter *Stepparent News,* following the same line of reasoning, calls the stepfamily to step "out of the nuclear family closet" and step into the world of reality. Five guidelines are offered to help the stepfamily do this.

1. *Honestly confront yourself, your spouse, and all the children. Recognize that each has a past. That past includes ex-spouses, other parents, court decrees, and some pleasant and unpleasant memories. And it's a past that cannot be shared by everyone.*

2. *Don't be afraid to admit that you are a stepfamily. Admit it to yourself and others. Then you can go about creating your own positive identity. Everyone can grow.*

3. *Recognize the reality of the stepfamily relationships' potential. There is enough room for all the characters on the stepfamily stage. It's just that the curtain goes up before a script is written and the roles defined. There is an initial scramble of entrances, exits, and missed cues. Without a director and script, many stepfamilies flee back into that nuclear family closet, where they are type-cast, misunderstood, and misdirected. But stay out of the closet, and go on to Step 4.*

4. *Listen to the ambivalent feelings that abound in the stepfamily relationships. Everyone in the stepfamily longs to be accepted and liked. Everyone also resents the invasion of someone into their space, at least part of the time. Ambivalent feelings are normal, psychologically healthy, and sometimes volatile in the stepfamily. Dealt with and listened to, ambivalent feelings can build relationships. They are ignored in the nuclear family closet.*

5. *As one unique stepfamily, begin to work on a script that meets the needs of the members of your stepfamily. Let each person take direction and responsibility for his part in the destiny. Remember that there is enough room for everyone in the stepfamily: fathers, stepfathers, mothers, stepmothers, biological children, and stepchildren.*[3]

Anne Lorimer echoes the same sentiment when she says that second marriages are marriages with a past, complete with "ghosts." Somebody else shared the bed, cooked the dinner, and listened to your partner's dreams and yearnings. And that person is still around, often in regular contact with the new stepfamily through the children.[4]

Probably the most concise statement of the "cast of characters" problem comes from a teen-age girl. When asked what effect being part of a stepfamily had on her ideas of marriage and the family, she said that her children would have four grandparents on her side and, if she married someone who was part of a stepfamily, her children might even have eight grandparents or more, including the stepgrandparents.

Stepfamilies have more of everything: parents, children, grandparents, and households. With so large a cast of characters there is a strong chance for discontinuity and chaos, as well as possibility for change and mixed communications. The crucial task for stepfamilies is learning how to cope with all these extras.[5]

The Readymade Family. "The impact of readymade families on remarriages is overwhelming," writes Elizabeth Einstein in *Human Behavior* magazine. She points out that several years of privacy often exist in a first marriage during which time a couple can get to know each other and plan the future together.[6]

The readymade family presents the new bride and groom with a situation that is absent in the natural family. Dependent children are *immediately* clamoring for their needs to be met. Often the new couple is not able to enjoy the newness and excitement of their relationship sexually because of the ever-present children, who may be old enough to be aware of what's going on in the bedroom.

Each person in the stepfamily, children included, brings into the stepfamily a sense of the way the family "ought" to function, complete with preconceived notions about the role of the biological parent, the stepparent, the biological children, and the stepsiblings. For example, the biological parent and child may think that the child "has" to obey the parent but that obedience to the stepparent is another matter. On the other hand, the stepparent may feel that he or she is as much a parent as the biological parent and therefore equal in authority.

This sense of "oughtness" or "rightness" about the family system creates unspoken expectations about the role and behavior of the others in the family. When these are disappointed, anger and resentment begin to poison the new family.

Readymade families also are usually contaminated with anger, guilt, jealousy, value conflict, misperceptions, and fear. These conflicts are often played out destructively, with sides being chosen by the immediate and extended stepfamily and sometimes the former spouses, who secretly desire to see the new family fail.

The readymade family also is riddled with problems of real or imagined disloyalty. An essential feature of family living, whether it be a natural family or stepfamily, is a sense that "we're all pulling together and supporting each other." Some things are the private business of the family and for the family's ears alone.

The readymade family produces a conflict of loyalty. Parents often feel in conflict between loyalty to their new spouses and the needs of their children (and sometimes their former spouses). Children feel torn between two biological parents whom they love and the two new families that these divorced parents have established. A mature adult has a difficult enough time with loyalties, let alone a child who doesn't really understand what is happening.

A Word of Caution

The "experts" make quite a good case for the "differentness" of stepfamilies. But I think a word of caution is in order here. It is possible that the "sameness myth" which they are trying to dispel may be replaced by another myth—*the myth that the natural family and stepfamily are so different that few of the rules fol-lowed in natural families can be applied to stepfamilies.* I repeat, this is a *myth*.

Writers on the subject are beginning to recognize the dangers of such a myth. Consider, for example, the principle of a united parental front. This is needed in both the natural family and the stepfamily. Says Elizabeth Einstein, "Experience and research prove that as leaders of the new troop, the new husband and wife set the tone for the stepfamily. If a successful job is to be accom-plished, the parenting styles of both adults must yield to change and compromise so that the children are presented with a united front."[7]

Though he acknowledges that readymade families have unique problems, Frank Halse, Jr., family therapist at the Child and Family Service Agency of Syracuse, New York, says that the effectiveness of the parent/stepparent team "will stem from basi-cally the same parenting techniques that work within primary [natural] families."[8] That is my emphasis in this book. While we must allow for the problems that are unique to stepfamilies, let's be careful to apply and adapt to stepfamilies as many principles of good parenting and family relationships as we can cull from our experience with natural families.

This emphasis will be unfolded in the coming chapters. But before we go any further into the theory and practice of step-parenting, let's take a look at *you* as a stepparent or potential stepparent. The next chapter offers "The Stepparent Test" and gives you an opportunity to evaluate yourself and your spouse as leaders or potential leaders of the new troop.

2.

The Stepparent Test

This is not a test in the formal sense—a statistical analysis. It is more a tool to open discussion between the stepparent and the biological parent—to talk about the issues you are or will be facing as a stepparent. It also offers a fair estimate of your success as a stepparent. The statements in the test do not deal with issues that every marriage might face, like your spouse's choice of friends. They deal with stepparenting.

The test may be taken by a person who is already a stepparent or is about to become one. For simplicity, however, the statements are made as though you are a stepparent already. If you are not yet a stepparent, simply make the necessary mental adjustment as you read each statement. For example, "I think that I am patient with my stepchild(ren)" would read, "I think that I would be patient with my future stepchild(ren)."

Both you and your spouse (or fiancé) should take the test. Do not consult each other as you take it. It is important that both of you say exactly how you feel. It is not important whether or not you *should* feel as you do. The important thing is for both of you to know how the other feels about the statements made in the test. You will have an opportunity to discuss your answers later.

Try to answer "yes" or "no" and avoid "undecided" as much as possible. This way you will be able to make a better assessment and will have more to discuss.

How to Do the Test

Take a sheet of paper and number it from 1 to 44. Respond to each statement in one of four ways: Yes, Undecided, No, or Not Applicable (N/A). "Not applicable" means that the statement does not apply to you. For example, if you have children and are marrying someone who has no children, the first statement in the test does not apply to you: "I think that I am patient with my stepchild(ren)." You would answer "N/A" since you have no stepchildren. It is your spouse who has the stepchildren. Remember, answer on the basis of how *you feel*. Don't try to answer the way you think each question *should* be answered.

The Stepparent Test

	Yes	Unde-cided	No	N/A
1. I think that I am patient with my stepchild(ren).	—	—	—	—
2. I think that my spouse is patient with his/her stepchild(ren), my biological child(ren).	—	—	—	—
3. I think that I can be happy being a stepparent to my spouse's child(ren).	—	—	—	—
4. The words *interest* and *commitment* describe my attitude toward the child(ren) for whom I am stepparent.	—	—	—	—
5. I am concerned that in the future I may be expected to care for an additional stepchild whether I want to or not.	—	—	—	—
6. I expect to be appreciated by my stepchild(ren).	—	—	—	—
7. I expect to be loved by my stepchild(ren).	—	—	—	—
8. I want to have children by my new spouse.	—	—	—	—
9. I feel confident that I can be an effective stepparent.	—	—	—	—
10. I am confident that my spouse can be an effective stepparent.	—	—	—	—

	Yes	Unde-cided	No	N/A

11. I think that the noncustodial parent will make my job of stepparenting more difficult. ___ ___ ___ ___

12. I believe that my spouse is likely to take sides with his/her child(ren) against me, the stepparent. ___ ___ ___ ___

13. I believe that my spouse, the stepchild(ren)'s parent, will support me in my role as stepparent. ___ ___ ___ ___

14. I think that my spouse puts his/her child(ren) ahead of me when it comes to attention, affection, time, or activity. ___ ___ ___ ___

15. I believe that my spouse shows more favor toward his/her own child(ren) than toward mine. ___ ___ ___ ___

16. I expect that stepparenting will be an easy job. ___ ___ ___ ___

17. I really want to be a stepparent. ___ ___ ___ ___

18. I think that my spouse really wants to be a stepparent. ___ ___ ___ ___

19. I wish that my stepchild(ren) did not live in the same house with me. ___ ___ ___ ___

20. I think that my spouse would rather not have my child(ren) live with us. ___ ___ ___ ___

21. I basically like kids. ___ ___ ___ ___

22. I think that my spouse basically likes kids. ___ ___ ___ ___

23. I think that I could raise a stepchild, but I'm really not that interested. ___ ___ ___ ___

24. I think that my spouse could raise a stepchild, but he/she really doesn't seem that interested. ___ ___ ___ ___

25. I feel that I am being pressured into being a stepparent against my wishes. ___ ___ ___ ___

26. I eagerly look forward to being a stepparent because it will bring me closer to the child(ren)'s parent whom I'm marrying. ___ ___ ___ ___

		Yes	Unde-cided	No	N/A
27.	My stepchild(ren) come(s) between me and the parent, my spouse.	—	—	—	—
28.	I feel comfortable about stepparenting a child of any age or sex.	—	—	—	—
29.	My spouse runs down his/her former spouse in front of his/her child(ren).	—	—	—	—
30.	I think that the stepparent in this family runs down the biological parent of the same sex (e.g., stepmother runs down the biological mother).	—	—	—	—
31.	I think that the stepfather feels overwhelmed by having to support two families.	—	—	—	—
32.	I think that the wife in this family, who works outside the home, resents it because she is having to support her husband's former family.	—	—	—	—
33.	I think that the wife in this family resents her husband's payments of alimony or child support to his former wife.	—	—	—	—
34.	I think that the current wife uses money as a measure of the husband's love and loyalty.	—	—	—	—
35.	I think that the husband's will favors the ex-wife and/or his child(ren) more than the present wife.	—	—	—	—
36.	I feel uncomfortable about the way the stepfather relates to his stepdaughter(s) sexually.	—	—	—	—
37.	I think that my new spouse is harsher in discipline with my child(ren) than with his/her child(ren).	—	—	—	—
38.	I think that I can discipline my stepchild(ren) without the biological parent interfering.	—	—	—	—
39.	I believe that I will have trouble being a stepparent while my own child(ren) is (are) living with someone else.	—	—	—	—

	Yes	Unde-cided	No	N/A
40. I believe that my stepchild(ren) will interfere with my developing a strong relationship with the biological parent, my spouse.	—	—	—	—
41. I think that my spouse's conversation usually centers on his/her child(ren) and rarely on us as husband and wife.	—	—	—	—
42. I think that my possessions are respected by my stepchild(ren).	—	—	—	—
43. I think that my living space is respected by my stepchild(ren).	—	—	—	—
44. My spouse should be willing to give up his/her child(ren) if I as a stepparent can't handle the job of stepparenting.	—	—	—	—

Numerical Score _____

Agree/Disagree Score _____

Scoring

You will compute two scores on this test. They are a Numerical Score, obtained from the scoring key at the end of this chapter, and an "Agree/Disagree" Score from your spouse.

Numerical Score. Compare your answer sheet with the scoring key. Put the number value for each answer in the margin next to your answer. For example, if you answered no. 1 "Yes," put a 3 in the margin of your answer sheet next to the first question. Please note that "Yes" and "No" answers don't all have the same value. If you answered "Yes" to no. 5, the score is 1. If you answered "N/A," put a zero (0) next to the statement. Add up the numbers. This is your subscore.

Next, add the number of times you responded "N/A." Multiply that by 3 and add that amount to your subscore, which will give you your final score.

Let us say, for example, your subscore is 93, obtained from the scoring key. Now suppose that eight times you marked "N/A." Multiply that by 3 and you have 24. Add the 24 to the 93 and you have a score of 117. The highest possible score is 126. (Two of the statements are for discussion only.)

Let's take a look at how you view the current or future success of your stepparenting:

126–115 Optimistic outlook
114–105 Somewhat doubtful outlook
104–below Very pessimistic outlook

Obviously you will be looking for a high numerical score. In considering your score you should remember that it does not simply reflect on your abilities as a stepparent. It also reflects on the expected cooperation from the biological parents, the children, and the rest of the cast of characters who will influence the stepparenting process. A low score, therefore, does not necessarily reflect on you the stepparent, but on the whole cast of characters in the stepfamily.

Agree/Disagree Score. Let's look at the test from another angle. Do you see yourself as a member of this stepfamily the same way your spouse sees you? For example, the first statement says, "I feel that I am patient with my stepchild(ren)." Let's say that you answered "Yes." You honestly believe you are patient. How does your *spouse* feel about this? Does he or she think you are patient? To find out, you should exchange answer sheets, and on the left side next to the number of the statement, your spouse should write an "A" if he or she agrees and a "D" if he or she disagrees.

But let me caution you not to fall into arguing over who is right! One answer is not right and the other wrong. Your positions are *different from* not *better than* each other's. You may want to read my book *Just Talk to Me*[1] for more on nonargumentative communication.

The purpose of the exercise is to help you see how your spouse's position may differ from yours. Remember, you are doing this, *not* to determine who's right, but to open the channels of communication on matters where you differ. You are to talk about these differences to achieve, not *agreement,* but *understanding.* You can't begin to solve problems until you understand and respect each other's point of view.

Now count up the number of times your spouse wrote "D." The lowest possible score is zero (0); the highest is 44. Obviously you will be looking for a low Agree/Disagree score.

Let's take a look at how closely your spouse agrees with you:

0–5 Close agreement
6–11 Moderate disagreement
12–above Serious disagreement

If there is moderate or serious disagreement, you can expect to have a lot of arguments over who is right and who is wrong when you talk about your stepfamily and stepparenting. If this happens, you need to sharpen your communication skills and learn the two basic rules:

1. Communicate for understanding rather than to determine who is right.

2. Communicate in a nonattacking and nondefensive manner.[2]

Your success at stepparenting will depend on your ability to talk about your disagreements *constructively*. Successful marriages and families are not without problems. They are successful because they talk about their disagreements constructively. Out of mutual respect and good will they resolve those disagreements.

Scoring Key

	Yes	Unde-cided	No	N/A
1.	3	2	1	0
2.	3	2	1	0
3.	3	2	1	0
4.	3	2	1	0
5.	1	2	3	0
6.	1	2	3	0
7.	1	2	3	0
8.	No right or wrong answer here. Your answer should agree with your spouse's.			
9.	3	2	1	0
10.	3	2	1	0

11. 1	2	3	0
12. 1	2	3	0
13. 3	2	1	0
14. 1	2	3	0
15. 1	2	3	0
16. 1	2	3	0
17. 3	2	1	0
18. 3	2	1	0
19. 1	2	3	0
20. 1	2	3	0
21. 3	2	1	0
22. 3	2	1	0
23. 1	2	3	0
24. 1	2	3	0
25. 1	2	3	0
26. 1	2	3	0
27. 1	2	3	0
28. 3	2	1	0
29. 1	2	3	0
30. 1	2	3	0
31. 1	2	3	0
32. 1	2	3	0
33. 1	2	3	0
34. 1	2	3	0
35. 1	2	3	0
36. 1	2	3	0
37. 1	2	3	0
38. 3	2	1	0
39. 1	2	3	0
40. 1	2	3	0
41. 1	2	3	0
42. 3	2	1	0
43. 3	2	1	0

44. No right or wrong answer here.
This is a discussion starter.

3.

Evaluating the Stepparent Test

It is important that you understand why I ask the questions I do in the Stepparent Test. In fact this test is more helpful if you understand their purpose. Remember that the test is not a statistical analysis but a tool to open discussion.

In this evaluation you will find at the end of each test statement page numbers in parentheses, like *(p. 39)*. The test statement is discussed on those pages. This gives you a ready reference to more reading on the issues that trouble you.

1. "I think that I am patient with my stepchild(ren)." The preferred answer is "Yes," for obvious reasons. Rearing children, whether your own or someone else's, takes patience. You also will want to look carefully at the Agree/Disagree (A/D) score. If you say you are patient, does your spouse agree with your estimate of yourself? You can avoid a lot of "I *am* patient/ You are *not*" arguments if you will *listen* to each other and understand why each of you feels as you do *(pp. 61, 88, 112)*.

2. "I think that my spouse is patient with his/her stepchild-(ren), my biological child(ren)." The preferred answer is "Yes." As with the first question, do you and your spouse agree? Suppose you say "No" and feel that he is not patient. He may disagree because he feels he is patient. Again, don't fall into arguing over who is right. Communicate for understanding *(pp. 37, 61, 112)*.

3. "I think that I can be happy being a stepparent to my spouse's child(ren)." The preferred answer is "Yes," but don't say it if you don't mean it. Some people become stepparents because the marriage is a "package deal": the children come with their parent. It is a tragic mistake to get into a package deal without carefully weighing the consequences *(pp. 37, 88, 112).*

4. "The words *interest* and *commitment* describe my attitude toward the child(ren) for whom I am stepparent." The preferred answer is "Yes," for obvious reasons. The A/D score is important. Does your spouse feel that you show interest and commitment? If not, why not? (See *pp. 38, 53, 108, 112.)*

5. "I am concerned that in the future I may be expected to care for an additional stepchild whether I want to or not." The preferred answer is "No." If you wrote "Yes," go slowly in developing the relationship if you are not already married. You should be very sure of the kind of "package" you're getting. Whether or not there is a remote chance that this will happen, you had better discuss it thoroughly *(p. 39).*

6. "I expect to be appreciated by my stepchild(ren)." You may be surprised, but the preferred answer is "No." Stepparents, teachers, and other nonparental authority figures should expect obedience and respect. But *appreciation* is a bonus if it comes. Children rarely appreciate anyone who frustrates their self-will, but authority figures must go ahead and do what is required of them even if they are not appreciated. Many *parents* are not even appreciated by their *own* children *(pp. 61, 71, 100, 102, 108).*

7. "I expect to be loved by my stepchild(ren)." The preferred answer is "No," for the reason given in number 6 *(pp. 61, 71, 100, 102, 108).*

8. "I want to have children by my new spouse." There is no right or wrong answer to this statement. You should both agree on whether or not you want a child of your own *(pp. 54, 71).*

9. "I feel confident that I can be an effective stepparent." The preferred answer is "Yes." If you appear confident, you will save yourself a lot of backtalk. Children test and exploit the weaknesses of authority figures, be they parents, stepparents, teachers, or others *(pp. 37, 65, 88, 108, 112).*

10. "I am confident that my spouse can be an effective stepparent." The preferred answer is "Yes." If you have doubts, say so. Just because your spouse makes a wonderful marriage partner doesn't mean that he or she will make a good stepparent. Be careful about idealizing this person's parenting abilities *(pp. 65, 108, 112)*.

11. "I think that the noncustodial parent will make my job of stepparenting more difficult." The preferred answer is "No." You will have enough to keep you busy as a stepparent without having to cope with an uncooperative noncustodial parent.

Note the A/D score here. If your spouse disagrees, you had better talk about it. Your spouse needs to understand the concern you feel whether or not he or she feels it's justified *(pp. 66, 72, 112)*.

12. "I believe that my spouse is likely to take sides with his/her child(ren) against me, the stepparent." The preferred answer is "No." If it is "Yes," and if your spouse disagrees, you should discuss it thoroughly. In my experience as a family therapist I find this to be one of the major causes of the breakup of stepfamilies *(pp. 54, 66–67, 71, 88, 108, 112)*.

13. "I believe that my spouse, the stepchild(ren)'s parent, will support me in my role as stepparent." The preferred answer is "Yes." You may not be the child's parent, but it ought to be made clear to the child what your role *is* as a stepparent and that the biological parent supports you in that role, just as he or she would support other authority figures in the child's life, such as teachers and policemen *(pp. 66–67, 108)*.

14. "I think that my spouse puts his/her child(ren) ahead of me when it comes to attention, affection, time, or activity." The preferred answer is "No." This, along with number 12, is a major cause for the breakup of stepfamilies. Often this happens because the biological parent feels guilty about the divorce and remarriage and feels he has to "atone" for his sin by "making it up" to the children.

Does your spouse agree or disagree on this? If you say he does and he says he doesn't, you're headed for another one of those unproductive "Yes, you do/No, I don't" arguments. *Listen to each other*. Communicate so you can *understand* and *respect* each other's feelings *(pp. 27, 36, 67, 71, 88)*.

15. "I believe that my spouse shows more favor toward his/ her own child(ren) than toward mine." The preferred answer is "No." If it is "Yes," you might want to look at the problem of guilt. Is he or she showing favoritism out of a sense of guilt? If your spouse disagrees, don't fall into an argument over who is right. Listen to each other. You need not agree, but you must listen to, understand, respect each other *(pp. 35–36, 71, 112).*

16. "I expect that stepparenting will be an easy job." The preferred answer is "No." A "Yes" answer may indicate naïveté in the stepparent or an idealized view of the stepfamily. Super-stepparents, beware! Be sure your spouse agrees that it will not be an easy job. If he or she thinks it will be easy, that person may be naïve or idealizing the situation *(pp. 61, 112).*

17. "I really want to be a stepparent." The preferred answer is "Yes," although I expect a "No" to appear frequently on this test. Again, it's the "package deal" problem: sometimes you have to take the kids along with the parent. Be honest if this is the case. You may save yourself much misunderstanding if you talk this out with the biological parent *(pp. 37, 54, 108, 112).*

18. "I think that my spouse really wants to be a stepparent." The preferred answer is "Yes," though a "No" is understand-able, for the same reason stated in number 17. Don't mistake your spouse's loving you for love for your children. Again, talk it out, especially if your spouse candidly admits that he or she really doesn't want to be a stepparent *(pp. 54, 108, 112).*

19. "I wish that my stepchild(ren) did not live in the same house with me." The preferred answer is "No," which means that you don't wish they'd get lost. It is hoped you are able to accept the stepchild as a member of the household and that the child also accepts you as a member of the household. Be honest in your answer, particularly if you're not yet a stepparent. Are you really going to be able to take that stepchild into the house along with the child's parent? Don't be surprised if your spouse disagrees with your assertion that you accept the child. You may be saying all the right words, but your attitude may indicate something else *(pp. 39, 54, 71, 88, 108, 112).*

20. "I think that my spouse would rather not have my child(ren) live with us." This is where the spouse is the stepparent. The preferred answer is "No." You think the spouse does accept your child. But again, if there is conflict, the problem may be more in attitudes than words. The stepparent may say all the right words but carry a rejecting attitude *(pp. 54, 88, 108, 112).*

21. "I basically like kids." The preferred answer is "Yes." If you are to relate successfully to children as a parent, stepparent, teacher, or other authority figure, you have to like children. They are very sensitive to adults who are uncomfortable around them or can't tolerate them. Many times conflict with children rises out of a basic enmity toward them *(pp. 62, 65, 108, 112).*

22. "I think that my spouse basically likes kids." The preferred answer is "Yes," for the same reason given in number 21 *(pp. 62, 65, 108, 112).*

23. "I think that I could raise a stepchild, but I'm really not that interested." The preferred answer is "No," which means, "I could do it, and I'm interested in doing it." Sometimes people are able to do something, but they aren't interested. Consider a fifty-five-year-old man who has raised a family. He contemplates marrying a thirty-year-old woman with a five-year-old child. He thinks, "I could do it, but I've done my duty to God and society in raising kids." Be honest in answering this one. Don't take the child because this is the only way to get the child's parent *(pp. 39, 62, 65, 112).*

24. "I think that my spouse could raise a stepchild, but he/she really doesn't seem that interested." The preferred answer is "No," which means he or she could and is interested. The same observation applies here as in number 23 *(pp. 62, 65, 112).*

25. "I feel that I am being pressured into being a stepparent against my wishes." The preferred answer is "No." The focus must be on the marriage and the benefits of that relationship. The children will grow up and someday leave the household—we hope! You may have some trouble with the A/D score here. Your spouse may deny pressuring you about stepparenting; but if you feel it, you must make it clear why you feel that way. And these feelings should be respected *(pp. 39, 62, 65, 108, 112).*

26. "I eagerly look forward to being a stepparent because it will bring me closer to the child(ren)'s parent whom I'm marrying." The preferred answer is "No." The motive is wrong.

Children should not be used to bring the parents closer. This may happen, and usually does, in a well-adjusted family. But it happens only when the stepparents' and parents' relationship is strong in its own right *(p. 70)*.

27. "The stepchild(ren) come(s) between me and the parent, my spouse." The preferred answer is "No." Yet this is a major problem with stepfamilies. Often the child has a case of misguided loyalty. He may feel that the stepparent shouldn't be there; his biological parent should. If you answered "Yes," your spouse may disagree. You must talk this out, and your feelings on this matter must be understood *(pp. 35, 54, 71, 88)*.

28. "I feel comfortable about stepparenting a child of any age or sex." The preferred answer is "Yes." However, for example, it may be very difficult for a young woman who has never had children to suddenly become the stepmother of teen-age boys, particularly if she is only ten years older than they are. Even if the boys are young, she may come from a family that had no experience with boys *(pp. 39, 112)*.

29. "My spouse runs down his/her former spouse in front of his/her child(ren)." The preferred answer is "No." The parent who does this may unwittingly create problems for the stepparent. The child(ren), out of loyalty to the absent parent, may give the stepparent a difficult time. Your spouse may disagree with your evaluation out of self-defense. However, if you see it this way, you must get a hearing *(p. 101)*.

30. "I think that the stepparent in this family runs down the biological parent of the same sex (eg., stepmother runs down the biological mother)." The preferred answer is "No." Again, the stepparent who does do this is courting trouble. The stepchild, out of feelings of loyalty, will defend the absent parent and give the stepparent a hard time *(p. 101)*.

31. "I think that the stepfather feels overwhelmed by having to support two families." The preferred answer is "No." However, that is a common problem with stepfamilies and needs to be discussed. It is quite possible that the A/D score will reveal disagreement on this one *(pp. 39, 88)*.

32. "I think that the wife in this family, who works outside the home, resents it because she is having to support her husband's former family." The preferred answer is "No." As with number 31, this is a common resentment. It needs to be discussed, particularly if the answer is "Yes" or if the A/D score reveals disagreement *(pp. 83, 88)*.

33. "I think that the wife in this family resents her husband's payments of alimony or child support to his former wife." The preferred answer is "No." As with the previous two statements, money is a sensitive subject in stepfamilies. If the answer is "Yes" or the A/D score reveals disagreement, this needs to be discussed *(pp. 39, 54, 83, 88–89)*.

34. "I think that the current wife uses money as a measure of the husband's love and loyalty." The preferred answer is "No." When a man is supporting two families, the second wife often feels resentful about the amount of money that goes to the former wife and children. She will often measure her husband's love and loyalty by the amount of money he spends on her. If the answer is "Yes" or the A/D score indicates disagreement, this must be discussed. This problem can seriously damage the second marriage *(pp. 39, 72, 83, 88)*.

35. "I think that the husband's will favors the ex-wife and/or his child(ren) more than the present wife." The preferred answer is "No." What the husband does with his will and assets is often used as a measure of love and loyalty by the second wife. If the answer is "Yes," or the A/D score registers disagreement, this must be discussed *(pp. 71–72, 83)*.

36. "I feel uncomfortable about the way the stepfather relates to his stepdaughter(s) sexually." The preferred answer is "No," which means that you do not feel uncomfortable. If the answer is "Yes" or the A/D score reveals disagreement, it must be discussed. Incest is a major problem in American families. In stepfamilies sexual restraint is less than in biological families because there is no biological bond to be violated *(pp. 71, 95)*.

37. "I think that my new spouse is harsher in discipline with my child(ren) than with his/her child(ren)." The preferred answer is "No." This is another sensitive issue with stepfamilies. If the answer is "Yes" or the A/D score shows disagreement, talk about it *(pp. 88, 112)*.

38. "I think that I can discipline my stepchild(ren) without the biological parent interfering." The preferred answer is "Yes." The stepparent must never be told, "You're not my real parent. You can't discipline me." The stepparent can and should be a disciplinarian together with the biological parent. Discuss this in depth if the answer is "No" or if there is disagreement on the A/D score *(pp. 54, 66, 112)*.

39. "I believe that I will have trouble being a stepparent while my own child(ren) is (are) living with someone else." The preferred answer is "No." Often, out of feelings of guilt, the stepparent will (1) do a poor job of stepparenting, (2) attempt to gain custody of his or her child(ren), or (3) divorce the second spouse and go back to his or her original family *(pp. 37, 54)*.

40. "I believe that my stepchild(ren) will interfere with my developing a strong relationship with the biological parent, my spouse." The preferred answer is "No." Often a child, out of loyalty to the absent biological parent, will interfere with the development of a strong relationship between the stepparent and the child's biological parent *(pp. 35, 55, 71)*.

41. "I think that my spouse's conversation usually centers on his/her child(ren) and rarely on us as husband and wife." The preferred answer is "No." Two issues are involved here: loyalty and the primary relationship. Unfortunately the biological parent's sense of loyalty to his or her child(ren) and a weak sense of a primary relationship with the stepparent is revealed in this type of conversation *(pp. 55, 72, 88)*.

42. "I think that my possessions are respected by my stepchild(ren)." The preferred answer is "Yes." Territorial aggression is always a sensitive issue, particularly in stepfamilies. It includes possessions as well as living space *(pp. 88, 112)*.

43. "I think that my living space is respected by my stepchild(ren)." The preferred answer is "Yes." Here we extend the issue of "territory" from possessions to living space *(pp. 88, 112)*.

44. "My spouse should be willing to give up his/her child(ren) if I as a stepparent can't handle the job of stepparenting." A right or wrong answer is not suggested here. This is a discussion starter. The purpose of this statement is to test the sensitive areas of the primary relationship, loyalty, and parental guilt *(p. 51)*.

4.

Guilt: The Great Spoiler

Rusty and Meg were deeply in love when I met them. Yet they were so unhappy with their marriage, the second for both of them, that they were considering divorce. What was wrong?

Meg came to the point quickly. "Rusty, my two daughters, and I get along beautifully by ourselves. But when Rusty's children enter the picture, our relationship falls apart." Rusty's daughter and two sons lived with their mother, but they visited Rusty and Meg every weekend. In recent months the regularity had fallen off. Their presence created such an explosive atmosphere in the home that something had to be done.

"Meg becomes an entirely different person when my kids are around," said Rusty. "It was fine if *I* wanted to visit with my kids, but she would make herself scarce until they were gone."

Meg admitted this was so. "It's purely visceral. My head tells me I should accept Rusty's children and be pleasant to them for the weekend; but the moment they hit the house, my stomach goes into a knot, and I want to get as far from them as I can.

"To put it gently, they simply are not nice children. They are rude, selfish, and inconsiderate. Rusty overlooks it and says that I should too. But I can't. What is more, my daughters are treated badly by them. It breaks my heart to see them be so polite and try to make Rusty's kids feel welcome and get nothing but discourtesy in return."

Rusty agreed that this did happen. He also had to admit that he really liked Meg's children more than his own—and even got along better with them. But Rusty was angry that Meg couldn't bring herself to make it a family weekend and be involved with him and his children. She completely disengaged. She either left the house or stayed in her room. When she had to be around them, she was cold and distant.

"These are *my* kids," said Rusty. "The least she can do is share a little of herself with them."

What was the problem here? There were several, but the one that created most of the problem was guilt—primarily Rusty's and to some degree, Meg's. By not coming to grips with his own feelings of guilt, Rusty tried to cope by insisting that Meg help him create a happy family scene with his children.

Rusty carried a lot of guilt about his children. He felt that he hadn't done a very good job raising them. He had spent too much time at work and not enough with his family. Now he had three rude and inconsiderate children as a legacy. He was a success as a businessman but a failure as a family man.

Furthermore, he felt guilty for liking Meg's children more than his own. They were decent children and gave him far more respect and consideration than did his own.

Finally, he felt guilty for "abandoning" his children. It was bad enough that he had done a poor job of raising them, but then he walked out on them and their mother as well!

Even though Rusty denied it, I believe he secretly felt that if he exposed them to Meg and her children, some decency would rub off on them. But it wasn't happening, mainly because Meg wanted nothing to do with them, and their father was still too indulgent out of guilt.

Rusty never did come to terms with his guilt. He continued to insist that the problem was not his guilt but Meg's unwillingness to make his children's visits a happy family time. His dogged insistence at this point finally led to a deterioration in the marriage and ultimately a divorce.

Such stories are not uncommon. Stresses that exist in the stepfamily are often magnified by a feeling of failure. It's no wonder that the divorce rate for stepfamilies is higher than that of first-marriage families—40 percent compared with 33 percent for the "first married."[1]

Guilty Parents

As we have observed above, the biological parent often carries a load of guilt into his or her second marriage.

Divorce and Remarriage. Even though divorce and remarriage are becoming more common, they are still frowned on in conservative religious groups. Those who have remarried often report a feeling of isolation in the church. More specifically, they feel that they are second-class citizens for having divorced and remarried. Though they are welcome to fellowship with the church, their marital status does not permit them the same leadership opportunities as the first-married enjoy.

I am not arguing for or against this practice. Each church must decide the issue for itself. I only wish to describe the plight of the remarried. I will say more about the theological ramifications of guilt later in the chapter.

Not only do the remarried feel guilty before the church, they often feel guilty within the extended family. They wonder, "What will mother and dad say about my divorcing and remarrying?" It is particularly painful when you are the first one to be divorced in your family.

Putting Another Person Before Your Children. Another guilt provoker is your new spouse. You have "fallen in love" and have remarried. This person is very special to you. But this person is a stranger to your children. How can you expect your children to understand the place this "stranger" has in your life? More difficult than that is to expect them to understand that the husband/wife relationship is primary, *not* the parent/child relationship. How can you get them to understand that *this stranger* now is your primary affiliation even above *your own children*?

For the reader who may have a problem agreeing with my thesis of the husband/wife relationship's being primary, let me digress a moment. (Chapter 5, "We First: Making the Marriage the Primary Relationship," deals with this subject in greater detail.) I believe that the husband/wife relationship is primary because both the Bible and nature teach it. A child *leaves* father and mother and establishes a new family with a spouse. The entire aim of the Bible's view of marriage is toward the growing relationship of husband and wife (Eph. 5:22–33; 1 Peter 3:1–7) and the separation of the children from the parents (Gen. 2:24; Eph. 5:31).

Your goal in marriage is to strengthen the ties of the primary relationship, husband and wife, while you are loosening the ties with your children to prepare them for independence. In the natural family this is understood. But in the stepfamily it is often missed because the new spouse is viewed as an interloper who has no right to claim the affection, loyalty, and primary place in the life of the biological parent. Whether it is a first or second marriage, unless the husband/wife relationship is the primary one, there is going to be trouble.

In my Stepparent Test I try to anticipate this. Several statements reveal this problem. For example, number 27 says, "My stepchild(ren) come(s) between me and the parent, my spouse." It is hoped the answer is "No" and such a thing is not permitted.

Number 40 says, "I believe that my stepchild(ren) will interfere with my developing a strong relationship with the biological parent, my spouse." Again, the answer should be "No."

If the answer is "Yes," I hope that the parent and stepparent will discuss the problem constructively.

I Owe My Children. The flip side of the previous guilt trip is the feeling, "I owe my children." Here we look at the mistake of making the children and their needs primary. This takes two different courses—one for the custodial parent and another for the noncustodial parent.

The custodial parent often feels, "I owe my children a happy life because I have hurt them by divorcing their parent." But would you really have helped your child by remaining married? Jackie Chesner, who has three biological children and three stepchildren, says:

> It's much better for children to come from broken homes than to come from homes with constant fighting and lack of respect and love for one another.

These children are apt to grow up with problems and are likely to have a bad attitude toward marriage causing their marriages to be over before they even start.

The longer you prolong a divorce, when it is needed, the harder it will be for the child to accept.

Stop and ask yourself, "Is this the environment you want your children to be brought up in?" How could it possibly be with no love to teach them that a home should be a place where the children feel secure and loved.

Ask the opinion of your children before you make the final decision. You may be amazed at their response.[2]

If you're really "thinking of the children," you will give serious thought to the possibility that the divorce was much more wholesome for them than staying in the marriage. Family therapist James Framo suggests that a divorce may represent "a healthy step away from an earlier neurotic choice of a mate or an illusory means of solving an internal problem."[3] Perhaps the divorce actually helped you and your children break out of a neurotic pattern of behavior.

This matter of owing something to the children is touched on in the Stepparent Test, numbers 14 and 15. Number 14 says, "I think that my spouse puts his/her child(ren) ahead of me when it comes to attention, affection, time, or activity." If the answer is "Yes," it may arise from the parent's feeling that she or he owes something to the child(ren). If number 15 is also answered "Yes," it may reflect the same problem. That question reads, "I believe that my spouse shows more favor toward his/her own child(ren) than toward mine." The favoritism may rise out of the guilt feeling, "I owe my children."

The noncustodial parent tends to reveal his or her guilt a little differently. It is often expressed, from the new spouse's point of view, as his having too much contact with the former spouse and the children who are living with her.

In his book *What Every Man Should Know About Divorce,* Robert Cassidy says,

Many second wives resent the continuing relationship between their husbands and their husband's ex-wives. Now, you may deny that you have a relationship with your ex-wife, but every time you

*phone to check on visitation for the weekend, every time you pick up
the children at your ex-wife's house, you are facing a reminder of
your past life.*

*What can you do? Be businesslike. Treat your ex-wife as if she
were interviewing you for a job. Be formal and aloof. Most important, don't allow your feelings of attachment, if they still exist, to
show through. Be courteous at all times without fawning over her.
Keep the phone calls short and to the point. Don't linger over questions about the in-laws or old friends. Your curiosity may be killing
you, but if you want to keep relations with your new wife tranquil,
spend as little time as possible dealing with your ex-wife.*[4]

The noncustodial parent must realize that handling his guilt im-
properly can make his new spouse feel displaced by the former
spouse.

The Stepparent Test touches on this issue in at least four statements. Statement 3 says, "I think I can be happy being a stepparent to my spouse's child(ren)." A "No" answer may rise out
of feelings of guilt over the neglect of one's own noncustodial
children. How can you give of yourself freely to your new family
when you feel that you have treated badly the family you left
behind? Number 9 probes the same issue: "I feel confident that I
can be an effective stepparent."

Statement 17 says, "I really want to be a stepparent." A
"No" answer may indicate feelings of guilt over "the family you
left behind." Number 39 is after the same thing: "I believe that I
will have trouble being a stepparent while my own child(ren) is
(are) living with someone else." A "Yes" answer may reveal
guilt feelings.

It is not uncommon for a man to divorce his second wife and go
back to his first wife (who has custody of his children) because he
needs to feel fulfilled as a father. A case in point is the stepfather
who felt unaccepted by his stepchildren and divorced his second
wife to remarry his first wife. He really didn't love the first wife
and he hated to leave his second wife, but he needed to be
fulfilled as a father and this need was not met in the stepfamily.

Needless to say, the return to the first marriage did not work.
All of the old problems surfaced again with his first wife. He
enjoyed being a custodial father again, but he still could not get

along with his first wife. Finally, he divorced her again and asked the second wife to take him back. But she wouldn't have him!

I Just Don't Like These Children. Another guilt trip the stepparent may have is his or her dislike for the new stepchildren—or any children for that matter. This was Meg's problem. She simply couldn't stand Rusty's children.

Why did Meg get into this in the first place? Certainly she knew Rusty's children before she married him. Meg had a couple of answers to that question.

First, she would be a noncustodial stepparent. She thought she could handle that. The most she would have to see Rusty's children was every other weekend, a week in the summer, and either Thanksgiving or Christmas.

The second reason Meg married Rusty, even though she didn't like his children, is that it was a "package deal." Whether you like it or not, your spouse's children come with him or her as part of the package. Parents cannot divorce their children; and even when the children live with the other parent, the children still have an impact on the life and marriage of the noncustodial parent and stepparent. Most stepparents are not aware of how great that impact is nor are they prepared to deal with it. Meg felt terribly guilty for feeling as she did, but that's where she was. I believe this marriage could have worked if Rusty had made his relationship with Meg the primary one and had looked forward to the day when his children would make families of their own. He complicated things by making himself vulnerable to his children's and former wife's manipulations, something I'll say more about shortly.

The Stepparent Test attempts to identify this problem. Number 4 says, "The words *interest* and *commitment* describe my attitude toward the child(ren) I am to stepparent." A "No" answer may be due to a dislike for this child. Don't let guilt feelings stand in the way of your discussing this, especially if you have not yet become a stepparent! And don't let anyone say, "You shouldn't feel that way." Admit that, "I do feel that way, and I'm not going to feel guilty because of it." Let's be realistic: *Not all children are likeable!* There have been times when I haven't liked *my own* children—and the feeling has been mutual!

Test statement 5 says, "I am concerned that in the future I may be expected to care for an additional stepchild whether I want to or not." If the answer is "Yes," again, talk it out. It must be discussed with a clear understanding of the husband/wife relationship's being the primary one. I believe that a lot of problems and guilt feelings in second marriages can be avoided if the primary relationship is clearly understood. For more on that, see the next chapter. See also test statements 19, 23, 25, and 28. The "package deal" problem ought to be discussed with numbers 19, 23, and 25. Number 28 looks for more specific problems. You may be comfortable stepparenting girls, but uncomfortable rearing boys. Likewise, small children may delight you, but teenagers infuriate you.

Guilt and Money. Money problems are common to every family, but stepfamilies seem to have more trouble in this area than natural families. And out of money problems comes guilt.

Three statements on the Stepparent Test probe this problem. Number 31 reads, "I think that the stepfather feels overwhelmed by having to support two families." When a man remarries, he often carries some financial responsibility for his first family as well. It's difficult to support one family, let alone two, and it can be overwhelming. The new wife may resent these obligations, and the husband may feel guilty because he is not meeting her needs financially. Likewise, the second wife may feel guilty for her resentments because she knew before she married the man that he had these obligations.

Even though talking won't remove the obligations, it may help the couple come to terms with their resentments and guilt. Feeling appreciated and understood by each other makes the burden a little easier to carry.

Number 33 looks at the problem from the wife's point of view: "I think that the wife in this family resents her husband's payments of alimony or child support to his former wife." Again, talk it out. Understand and empathize with each other.

Number 34 ties in with the same problem. "I think that the current wife uses money as a measure of the husband's love and loyalty." Often, the second wife does this because of her resentment over the money that goes to the former wife. She often feels jealous—and then guilty because she knew he had these obligations before she married him.

Both husband and wife need to understand and empathize. He needs to understand that her feelings often rise out of insecurity, both emotional and financial. Understanding and caring go a long way to making the problems easier to handle.

Guilty Children

Parents are not the only ones who feel guilty and cope with it inappropriately. The inappropriate behavior of children often arises out of feelings of guilt.

Guilt Over the Divorce. One common problem children in the stepfamily face is guilt over their parents' divorce. Even when the children are told that they had nothing to do with the divorce, feelings of guilt often persist. They sometimes think, "Okay, maybe I wasn't at fault for breaking up mom and dad, but I could have done *something* to prevent it." And then across the mind flash all those past scenes in which mom and dad yelled at them for their poor behavior and failures. The child thinks, "Maybe if I had done better in school, had been more obedient, had cleaned up my room, had been more considerate, I would have made the burden on mom and dad easier. Maybe *I* was the straw that broke the camel's back. Mom did scream at me once, 'You're driving me to the nuthouse!' And I'll never forget dad telling me how ungrateful I was."

Parent, you don't know how many times those scenes will be played over and over in your child's mind and offer the conclusion that he or she is guilty for pushing you over the brink.

Guilt and Loyalty. Every family teaches the need for loyalty. The biological bonding process and many myths that surround it strengthen that sense of loyalty: "Children love their parents; parents love their children."

When a family breaks up in divorce, the children's sense of loyalty to the biological parents becomes even stronger. It is a way of maintaining that bond even though the family has broken up.

A common problem in the stepfamily is the rejection of the stepparent by the stepchild. The stepchild may be well-mannered and well-behaved for the custodial biological parent but treat the stepparent badly. This behavior often arises out of the child's sense of loyalty to the absent parent. He reasons, "If I am nice to my stepmother, my real mother may feel that I don't love her, and this will hurt her." Not wanting to be guilty of that, the child may simply ignore stepmother or be downright unpleasant.

I'll get into this more when I discuss the roles of the stepparents and stepchildren. But the stepparent should be aware that the child's poor behavior may be traced to feelings of guilt.

This also explains why a child will often defend a parent's bad behavior. Ginny's husband left her for another woman. Ginny's son, who is in his early twenties, wanted to know why his father left. He was concerned over his dad's well-being, especially with the holidays coming up. When mother told him that dad was living with another woman, the young man said, "I'm sorry to hear that." Then he brightened up and said, "At least dad won't be alone at Christmas."

His mother was devastated! "Haven't I taught my son better than that—to be so casual about adultery? Does he *approve* of his dad's behavior?" Ginny needed to understand loyalty and the need to avoid the guilt that comes with finding flaws in one's parents.

Theological or Psychological Guilt

Fran attended church regularly with her teen-age daughter, Anne. Fran's husband never went with them because he had "no interest in religion," to use his words.

Though their marriage had been in trouble for years, Fran wasn't prepared for the shocking revelation that her husband had been having homosexual affairs for years and now had decided to leave her and "come out of the closet." As painful as it was, the broken marriage and Fran's disillusionment with her husband was put behind her, and she rebuilt her life.

In time she met a widower in her church and married him— with her pastor's blessing. Her pastor took the position that her former husband was an adulterer and had left the marriage, leaving her free to remarry.

Many members of the church didn't see it that way. Divorce

and remarriage were sins, no matter what the circumstances. They believed that Fran and her new husband Herb were living in adultery and were sinners in God's eyes. So when Fran and Herb began to have trouble with Anne, there wasn't much sympathy. In fact, some of the church members made matters worse by siding with Anne against "her sinful parents." The alliance between Anne and her supporters became so destructive to the family that Fran and Herb moved to another church, while Anne stayed put.

The situation devastated Fran. Deep feelings of guilt swept over her. She felt that she had ruined Herb's life by marrying him and exposing him to hurt from the people of his own church. Even though her pastor assured her that she was guiltless according to Scripture, she *felt* guilty. Herb, likewise, assured her that he knew what he was getting into, and he had a responsibility for the decision to marry as well as she.

Guilt can be "theological" or "psychological." Theological guilt is the consequence of a broken law, divine or human. Psychological guilt is the subjective feeling of guilt even though the head says, "Not guilty."

Are Divorce and Remarriage Unforgivable Sins? I deal with the issue of biblical grounds for divorce in my book *But I Didn't Want a Divorce,* so I won't go into it here.[5] But this much I must say to the remarried who labor under feelings of guilt. Let's say that you really are "theologically guilty." You believe that you really have broken God's law by divorcing and remarrying. Is this an *unforgivable* sin in God's eyes? I know of no unforgivable sins in the Bible, except the rejection of Christ. And certainly you will not correct the sin by divorcing the second person you have married and returning to the former marriage. More often than not a return to the former marriage is impossible even if you desire it.

I am not saying that Fran was guilty. Nor am I suggesting that you are guilty, because I don't know your circumstances. What I am saying is that even if you feel you *have* broken God's law, God graciously offers you relief through His Son Jesus Christ, who died on the cross to satisfy God's judgment against your sin. All you need do to have *your* guilt removed is to accept that sacrifice for your sins. God accepts the sacrifice of Christ as payment for the penalty due us. Won't you?

I am not saying by this that divorce and remarriage is *ipso facto* a sin. I am saying that *if* it is, God has provided a gracious remedy for it.

Beware of the Guilt Manipulators. Let's say that you believe you are guilty of sin and have accepted Christ as God's remedy, but you still feel guilty. You are more likely suffering from psychological guilt. This is guilt that arises out of past conditioning by parents and "significant other" adults. Adults often control children through guilt. When the child grows up, he finds that he still has the same problem—people continue to control him by making him feel guilty, even though his head knows better.

You need to beware of manipulators, especially those who manipulate by guilt. Guilt manipulators try to control you by making you believe you are behaving badly. By convincing you of this, they hook your feelings of guilt. They do this to control your "bad" behavior—when they make you feel guilty, you'll stop doing what they don't like.

Anne tried this on her mother, Fran. Anne said, "I don't have to listen to you or Herb. In the first place, he's not my real father, and in the second place, the two of you are living in sin!"

This threw Fran into a tailspin. Anne controlled her mother by making her feel guilty, and Fran encouraged this manipulation by backing off. With a little coaching, Fran regained control. The next time Anne tried her guilt manipulation, Fran said, "I'm not sure that Herb and I have sinned by remarrying. But even if we have, hear this. You may not forgive us, but God does. And if you're going to live in the same house with us, you're going to clean up your self-righteous act and show some respect and obedience. And if you can't, you may find somewhere else to live." Anne got the message. Though she continued to keep Herb at a distance, she changed her attitude immediately.

If you find that feelings of guilt hang on, you may need professional help. You will find guidance on this in the last chapter. But in the meantime, remember this. When God forgives you and you do not, you make yourself greater than God. How dare you not forgive when He does!

5.

We First: Making the Marriage the Primary Relationship

Dear Abby:
Judy and I have been married for one month, and I have already filed for divorce. This is the second marriage for both of us.
The problem is Judy's 16-year-old daughter, Lynne. Lynne told her mother that if she stayed married to me, she'd go live with her father. Judy doesn't want Lynne to live with her father because he drinks. Also, Lynne threatened to get pregnant just for spite.
Judy insists that she loves me. She says she doesn't want a divorce, and the solution would be for me to move out and get a separate apartment near here for two years until Lynne was 18.
Abby, I love Judy more than any woman I've known, but what kind of marriage would we have living in separate apartments?
Please tell me what do do.–UNHAPPY IN VA

DEAR UNHAPPY: Move out. But as long as you love Judy, don't push for a divorce until you are positive that you really want one. Lynne is blackmailing her mother, who can't be blamed for doing what she thinks is best for her daughter. Both the daughter and mother need counseling. I recommend it.[1]

This excerpt from Abigail Van Buren's well-known column presents a problem common to parents with older teen-agers. Abby's advice is basically sound.

"Unhappy in VA" should move out. He will not convince Judy that she is wrong. She is tied into a destructive bond with her daughter that permits blackmail. But blackmail doesn't work unless a person makes himself vulnerable to it, which is what Judy is doing.

What makes Judy think that things will be any different when Lynne is eighteen? The blackmail will continue over other issues. But the threat will be the same: "If you don't . . . then I will. . . ." Judy is actually teaching Lynne the art of blackmail by submitting to her. Lynne will hone to perfection this art in her adult life unless Judy does something about it. What can Judy do? She can refuse to be blackmailed.

Judy's problem is that she doesn't want Lynne to live with her father because he drinks. I don't know that such a fate is worse than teaching Lynne to be a blackmailer. What is more, the consequences of her blackmail's exploding in her face (by going to live with her father) would make it unlikely that she would try this manipulation again.

As for the pregnancy, I don't know if she would really do it. But then again, pregnancy may be the price that Lynne has to pay to learn that she just doesn't control the lives of other people with threats.

"But what about the innocent baby?" you ask. The baby can be put up for adoption. It is unlikely that Lynne would want to keep it when she would just be getting pregnant out of spite.

Judy must tell Lynne, "Do whatever you have to do, but you will *not* control my life." She must tell Lynne that she is prepared for her to live with her father and to get pregnant. She will just have to do what she has to do.

This is what is known as "tough love," something that is regaining popularity among family therapists. Tough love means that you love the child enough to let him or her hurt. Out of that hurt comes the necessary corrective.

This is what God is doing with His chosen people Israel. He loves them enough to let them suffer from their rejection of Him and His Son Jesus Christ. And the Book of Hebrews reinforces this truth when it says, "Because the Lord disciplines those he loves, and he punishes everyone he accepts as a son" (Heb. 12:6).

I'll say more about "tough love" in my next chapter. I only want to point out that Judy's problem is that she has failed to respond properly to Lynne's blackmail. What is more, she did not grasp the principle that I am advancing in this chapter—the importance of making the marriage the primary relationship.

Theory of the Primary Relationship

By making the marriage "primary" I mean the following. In every family system, natural or step, part of the parents' task is to model good enduring husband/wife relations. What they *do* in relating to each other gives the child (or stepchild) an idea of what a good husband/wife relationship is like. No amount of education by the church or the school system can substitute for the impact made by the example of a good husband/wife relationship in the home.

A second part of the parents' task is to prepare the child (or stepchild) for his or her own independence and marriage, if the child so chooses. The entire movement of the family system is toward the strengthening of the husband/wife relationship and the preparation of the child for his or her own independence, spouse, and family. As a family you are to be moving in the direction of an *empty nest*.

You have heard of the "empty-nest syndrome"—the despair parents feel when the last child leaves home. I believe the best protection against this trauma is exactly what I advocate here—the strengthening of the husband/wife relationship and the preparation of the child for independence.

At the time of this writing I have one son left at home, Jonathan, age eighteen, a senior in high school. He is the last of four sons, three of whom are successful with families of their own.

My wife, Fay, and I dearly love Jon. His wit and thoughtfulness make him a delight to have around. But in spite of this, Fay and I are looking forward to the "empty nest." Over the past few years we have experienced a revival in our marriage, and we anticipate enjoying each other again without the encumbrance of children. My point is that the natural process of emptying the nest is not a trauma for us but offers the opportunity of a new and exciting future for our marriage.

Enter the Stranger. The same dynamic must develop in step-families. Unfortunately, divorce and remarriage complicate things. Here is a divorced mother with devoted children. They have "lost" their father in divorce. Realistically, visitation or even joint custody doesn't offer the same opportunity to be with dad as having mom and dad living together and enjoying each other. Then a *stranger* enters the picture. What *right* does this stranger have to capture mother's love and devotion? Neither mother nor the children say anything, but they *feel* the tension. And the feeling turns to pain when mom wants to spend more time with this stranger than with her own children!

This feeling often produces guilt and an unwholesome reaction. Mother feels the need to assure the children that they will always have a place in her heart. But the children will not be appeased. So mother feels the need to give more assurances: "No, my dears. This stranger will not take me away from you. You will always have the first place in my heart!"

Wrong, wrong, wrong! Indeed, the children need the assurance that mother will always be there. *But she must not overreact.* She must not tell the children that they are primary and that the stranger, her new husband, is secondary. What does this teach them about the nature of marriage and of family living? Do you want to tell them, "When you marry and have a family, put your children first and your husband second"? I hope not.

I am not talking about neglecting the children or casting them aside. And I am aware that there are times when a child is particularly distressed and therefore must come first in the order of time and priority in the family. Certainly, children need to feel loved and secure in the knowledge that they have a loving and warm home. But the philosophy of family life and the outlook parents are to take should be for the bond of husband and wife to grow stronger. The bond with the children will loosen, change, and mature as they become adults.

This positive relationship with the new family may be disrupted not only by the custodial parent, but also by the noncustodial parent. In the controversial book *Beyond the Best Interests of the Child,* the authors make a helpful statement along this line. They say that whether or not a parent without custody is to be legally allowed to visit his children should be solely at the discretion of the parent with custody. They go so far as to say that the absent parent—if the parent with custody so desires—should be legally prevented from seeing the children. They argue that this would enable the custodial parent and the new spouse to bring up the child without conflict from the now-absent parent. And I should add that it would enable the parent and stepparent to develop their relationship without interference from a perhaps angry or jealous former spouse who attempts to poison that relationship through the children. The authors maintain that court-ordained visitations are an official invitation to disrupt the unbroken continuity of the new family. They reason that conflicts of loyalty are common and normal under such conditions, and these have devastating consequences by destroying the child's positive relationship to the new family.[2]

The courts, trying to be fair to both biological parents, often create a chaotic situation. The child has neither the stability of the original natural family nor a stable stepfamily. The husband/wife relationship, whether in the natural family or stepfamily, is the keystone that maintains the integrity of the family system. Jeopardize that and the entire family structure comes tumbling down.

Why Did You Remarry? Sometimes the motivation for remarriage is the complicating factor. Why did you remarry?

Too often people remarry to provide a new parent for their bereft children. Such a motive is wrong. In the first place, you cannot give the child a ''new'' parent. In the child's mind mom and dad will always be mom and dad even if they are not living together, or one of them may have died.

The best you can hope for in remarriage is a significant adult leader of the opposite sex in the household who will be accepted as just that—a significant adult leader in the household. Your reason for remarrying should be *to provide yourself with a new spouse*. Your relationship with this person must be primary; your children's is secondary. Again, by primary I mean a bond that is strengthened with a view toward greater intimacy. By secondary I mean a bond that is gradually relaxed, changed, and matured with time whereby the child becomes an independent, self-sufficient adult.

Jan divorced her husband; and it seemed that from the day she announced the news to her daughters, they were trying to fix her up with a new man. To Jan this meant that the girls wanted a "new father." Nothing was further from the truth. The girls just didn't want mom to be alone.

Harry was in a different fix. He had three small children, a job, and not enough time to meet the demands on his life. He needed a mother for his children. The inevitable happened. Jan met Harry. Jan's daughters "needed" a new father, and Harry "needed" a mother for his three children. Thinking they were making a wise decision, they soon married.

Within the first month of the marriage Harry's patterns changed. Of course, if Jan had talked to his former wife, she would have found it was Harry's *usual* pattern. At quitting time on the job he found excuses not to come home. He said he had to stay at work, but he was bar-hopping with his buddies. The ugly reality of the situation was this: Once Harry found a mother for his children he returned to the pattern of behavior for which his first wife divorced him—a pattern of irresponsibility. His first wife thought she was getting even with him by giving him custody of the children, but he just found a new mother for them in Jan.

It didn't take long for Jan to get the picture. She had been chosen to be the new mother for Harry's children. And imagine her disappointment when she discovered that he not only expected her to be the mother of his children, but also he had no intention of being a stepfather to hers.

Friends and Lovers. Jean and Veryl Rosenbaum in *Stepparenting* make a strong plea for the primary relationship of husband and wife. They point out that friendship is the foundation of love in the marriage.[3]

This is something that children need to grasp. There is so much romantic nonsense and myth about marriage and the family. Our children need to understand that lovers should also be friends, something that was probably missing in the natural family before divorce and remarriage took place. In the stepfamily the couple has an opportunity to model a more constructive marriage. It's easy to love someone sexually, but the respect and caring that is shown in friendship alerts the children to the reality that there is a

49

lot more to love and marriage than "falling in love." People actually *work* at understanding each other. It doesn't just happen. Love is not just a feeling. It is caring behavior (1 Cor. 13). And this caring behavior is not preempted by the children. Yes, the parents care for the children. The children feel loved and secure. But obviously the parent/stepparent bond is something special and is different from the parent/child bond.

The Rosenbaums tell the story of Virginia and Bill who married after several years of being single parents. The marriage produced a combined family of seven: two adults and five children. After a year of marriage they were ready for a breakup. Virginia and Bill were confused. They couldn't understand why their love deteriorated.

Through counseling they discovered that their priorities were wrong. They permitted their jobs and their children to sap their strength to the point that they had nothing left for each other.

> *They discovered that from years of being single parents, they both paid too much attention to their teenagers. Actually, all the youngsters could have been self-reliant, but had grown used to depending on their parents for rides, advice, and daily care.*[4]

I'm not suggesting that the parent and stepparent become self-indulgent. But I am suggesting that they give the children the same message that is given to children in the natural family: "Please don't interrupt us now. Mom and dad have their needs, and we want this time to ourselves just to be with each other and enjoy each other. We'll get back to you." When the child sees how the biological parent establishes a friendship with this new mate, perhaps some of the confusion from the breakup of the first marriage may be dispelled. It is hoped the child will say, "Oh, *that's* what marriage is all about."

Giving Up Your Children

I'm not suggesting by what I say about the primary relation that the children go begging, though that sometimes happens—not only in the stepfamily. I've seen it happen in the natural family where the husband and wife are so involved in their own lives that the children are neglected. A balance is struck, in the well-adjusted family, between the parents' (and stepparents') needs and the children's needs. This teaches respect for the needs of others in family living.

The anecdote at the beginning of the chapter does, however, raise the issue of having to choose between child and spouse. This doesn't happen just in stepfamilies. I have seen it happen in natural families as well.

Al and Sandy had eight- and thirteen-year-old sons. By the time Sam reached age thirteen, his father considered him incorrigible. One day, at his wit's end, Al told Sam to get into the car. They drove to the local juvenile correction facility. In the parking lot Sam's dad told him, "I've had it with your insubordination and bad mouth. This is the last stop for you unless I see some change."

Sam got a sudden urge to behave, so dad broke off the confrontation. But mother was furious when she found out what had happened. She told Al, "There's nothing wrong with Sam. It's you and your unreasonable demands that are driving the boy to misbehave." Sandy aligned herself with Sam against dad. The marriage tottered on the brink of a fall, and Sam exploited it. Through counseling they finally resolved their situation, but not without much heartache from undercutting each other.

When a child is a disruptive force in the family, the parents (natural or step) must agree on a course of action and present to the child a united front. Whether the child stays at home or leaves should be a mutual decision of the parents, the outcome of which leaves *the marriage intact,* even though the family may be disrupted.

This is why I raise the issue I do in Stepparent Test, number 44: "My spouse should be willing to give up his/her child(ren) if I as a stepparent can't handle the job of stepparenting." There is no right or wrong answer because it is possible that the stepparent may be totally ill-equipped to stepparent or extremely unreasonable. But the issue is, Will this couple permit the stepchild to divide them or otherwise take the focus off the primary nature of their relationship? There are times when it is proper to move the child to another household so the parent and stepparent can get on with their lives. The child's move will come sooner or later. He is not a permanent fixture in the home. It may just come sooner than he thought!

Changing Houses in Midstream. When a couple marries for the second time, it is usually understood what the makeup of the stepfamily will be—you, me, so-many-of-my-children, and so-many-of-your-children. Yet sometimes a stepparent is thrown a curve. After several months or years of marriage, one of the former spouses reports that he or she can't live any longer with the custodial child. The child is being sent to live with the other parent. Or the child decides to change homes, as was the case with Lynne, who said she was going to live with her father *(pp. 44–45)*.

Let's say, for example, that a mother can't handle her teenage son any longer, so she says to him, "You can go live with your father." The son says angrily, "Okay, I will."

When the father hears of this he sympathizes with his son. If the son can't live with his mother, it is only natural that he live with his father. But wait a minute! What about the stepmother? Doesn't she have any say in this?

If the relationship between the boy's father and stepmother is primary, *she should definitely have a say*. The father would be wise to consult her on the matter and not *inform* her that his son is coming to live with them.

Perhaps she will agree that there is no other alternative and that she is willing to do this under certain conditions—like having a trial period. But whatever happens, she must be part of the decision and not just a rubber stamp for her husband's decision.

Remember, one day the teen-age boy will leave home and make it on his own. His stepmother and dad will be left to live the rest of their lives together. The father must not jeopardize this by unilaterally deciding that his son is coming to live with them.

This principle applies to all decisions that affect the family. Both the husband and wife should have a say in any major changes that affect the family, whether it be a job change, a move, or a child's coming to live with them. I have even had this problem with *natural* parents where the child was living with another relative and decided to come home to live. One parent wants the child to come home and the other parent does not. It must be a *mutual* decision if the marriage is to remain strong.

My Family and You. Another side of this problem is seen where only one parent brings children into the stepfamily. For example, a widower brings his two daughters into a stepfamily where the stepmother has never been married before. The situation is complicated by the decision (his) that they all will live in the house he and his daughters lived in. Even though the new stepmother doesn't like the idea of moving into the deceased woman's home, she goes along with it.

It's not long before her secret fears are confirmed. She realizes that this is not a new family made up of four people who had never been family before. She finds that she is thought of as a *replacement* for the deceased wife and mother. This is not a new family system. A family system already existed with father and daughters. Now the replacement, the stepmother, is expected to fit into this system and accept the living arrangements in the existing household.

Watch out before getting into something like this. The stepmother must *not* be thought of as a replacement. With her arrival *an entirely new family system is established* that experiences the new influence of a different person.

Of course the father and daughters will tend to continue old habits and patterns of interrelating. But a new mentality must be established. The stepmother is part of a *new* system and not a new cog in an existing system.

One thing that would have helped is for them not to have established their new family in the old family home. I know the arguments about the real-estate market and so on. But you pay a price to make your family system work. A new home emphasizes a new start. By moving into the old family home, the stepmother has to live with "ghosts" of the past.

Some Final Considerations. On the Stepparent Test I probe the matter of the primary relationship, and I want to point out here the particular statements that deal with it.

Number 4 talks about "interest" and "commitment" as a stepparent. A lack of these may indicate that you are really more interested in getting a new spouse than in getting more children.

There's nothing wrong with this. But you should face squarely the "package deal" problem. If you do get into a relationship where *you* feel that the marriage is primary and the children secondary, let your spouse know. Let him or her know that you are looking forward to the day when the children are gone and the two of you will be by yourselves.

Number 8 on the Stepparent Test relates to the issue of the primary relationship. Perhaps you want marriage but not any more children. Do make this clear to your spouse or fiancé if you have not married yet. Not everyone marries with a view of having children—either stepchildren or their own.

Number 12 raises the issue of taking sides. Often the stepparent takes sides because the marriage relationship is not primary. The primary relationship in such a family is between biological parent and child. Numbers 13 to 15 probe the same issue.

Numbers 17 to 20 should be looked at from the angle of the primary relationship. These four statements probe the place of the marriage and the place of the children or stepchildren.

Number 27 asks about the stepchild's coming between the biological parent and stepparent. If the issue of the primary relationship has been dealt with, this should be no problem. But if it is a problem, the parent and stepparent need to come to terms with the matter of the primary relationship.

Number 33 not only touches on resentments over money, but it also may touch on the issue of the primary relationship. Does the husband pay the alimony and/or child support and let it go at that? Or does he show more concern for his noncustodial children—and maybe even his former wife—than for his current wife? Numbers 34 and 35 relate to this as well.

Number 38 is a good test of the primary relationship. If the new husband and wife are one with each other, it will be demonstrated by a united front with the children.

Number 39 is another test of what is primary. Do not remarry if you are not going to make that relationship primary. Your spouse can feel that your heart really is with your children who do not live with you rather than with him or her. Certainly you will care about your children and show interest in their welfare. But is your new spouse primary?

Number 40 offers a similar problem, this time for the custodial stepchild. The biological parent *must* make it clear to the child that the new marriage is going to be given a lot of attention, and it will be a strong bond. This bond with grow stronger and endure; the bond with the child will part, change, and mature. They will relate more as good friends who lead their own lives. The child may be loyal to the absent parent but is not to interfere with this new relationship.

Number 41 touches on the same issue. The parent, wanting to give the child assurances that he or she is not being displaced by a stranger, may make the mistake of focusing most of the conversation on the parent/child relationship. Conversation about the marriage is important too. It serves as a model to the child of what a husband/wife relationship is all about.

The "One-Flesh" Concept of Scripture

The idea that the husband/wife relationship is primary is clearly stated in Scripture. In Genesis 2 we are told that God "made a woman" from man's rib and called her "wo-man" because she was taken from the man. By building a woman from the man, it seems that God intended to teach a union and communion between man and woman that does not exist in any other human relationship.

The comment by the sacred writer in Genesis 2:24 seems to reinforce this. He says that the husband/wife relationship has precedence over the parent/child relationship. Parent and child are to part ways. The new union of husband and wife is called "one flesh."

The intimacy of two personalities in marriage and the symbolism of intercourse are living reminders of the original one-flesh relation of our first parents. This is why I think that illicit sex is a unique sin (though not the *worst* sin). Paul says that all other sins are done outside the body, but this sin is very personal (1 Cor. 6:18). We sustain a *personal* injury that we do not experience from other sins.

Sexual intercourse produces a psychological vulnerability that other sins do not. When that psychological vulnerability is not protected by the commitment of marriage, people get hurt. I think the reason is that sexual intercourse is intended to symbolize the one-flesh union of our first parents, whose bodies actually were the same flesh.

The repetition of this "one-flesh" statement in Ephesians 5 is once again to reinforce the idea of union. Christ and the church are compared to a husband and wife. Paul also uses the analogy of a single body of which Christ is the Head and the church is His body.

The emphasis of Scripture is on the enduring and growing nature of the husband/wife relationship, while the parent/child relationship is only a temporary measure to prepare the children for adult life. The strength of a child's marriage comes largely from a good parental or stepparental model of marriage.

6.

Characteristics of a Helpful Stepparent

Though it is essential to respect the way in which stepfamilies differ from natural families, we must be careful not to let those differences excuse us from sound principles of interpersonal relations. Stepfamilies do face unique problems that natural families don't have. They come together as a readymade family with a varied history and sets of expectations, and the cast of characters is larger and often less willing to cooperate.

In this chapter I want to consider what characteristics should be found in a stepparent who is helpful and successful in that role. Actually, these characteristics should be present in *all* helpful adults, whether natural parents, stepparents, teachers, policemen, administrators, executives, or therapists. These principles come from Carl R. Rogers' article, "The Characteristics of a Helping Relationship," in which he makes that very point.[1]

I want to articulate these principles as they apply to stepparents and show how stepparents may use them as they run into problems that are unique to stepfamilies.

At least ten characteristics should mark the effective stepparent. The successful stepparent is—

- Congruent
- Nondefensive
- Not fearful of positive attitudes

- Able to be a separate person
- Able to grant others separateness
- Able to exercise accurate empathy
- Able to exercise nonpossessive warmth
- Nonthreatening
- Nonjudgmental
- Open to change

Congruent

Congruence is "getting our act together." What we get together are our words and actions.

For example, do you *say* that you are not annoyed when you *act* annoyed? Do you *say* that everything is fine when you *act* tense and testy? Many times we are incongruent because we are not aware of our feelings. In fact, we may take offense when someone says, "What's wrong?" As far as we are concerned, nothing is wrong simply because we are not aware of our behavior or feelings. But that other person, aware of our behavior, feels uneasy. What does our behavior mean? Is an explosion imminent? Has some disaster occurred?

If we become further annoyed because the person continues to press the question of what's wrong, we most certainly will see him draw back from us. Why? He is trying to establish a zone of safety. If he can't get enough information to determine what's wrong, then he'll create a safe distance just in case there's an explosion.

People instinctively play it safe around others by checking out behavior that appears threatening. In terms of helpful stepparenting, are you a *safe* person to be around? Can you be *trusted* not to explode unexpectedly and hurt those around you?

Often stepparents are offended when stepchildren treat them with distance. Is this your experience? Maybe you can't be trusted. Even though you are saying and doing all the right things, you are incongruent. You are tense and unhappy. You look like a bomb that is ready to go off. What you interpret as your stepchildren's lack of love and appreciation may be fear of you. You look and sound like a dangerous person.

The answer to the problem is awareness. If you seem tense and testy to your spouse or stepchildren, *get in touch with your feelings*. If you discover that you really do feel tense and are acting testy, don't defend it or attack them for their reaction to you. Become congruent, and share what's happening. For example, you might say, "Yes, I think you're right. I do feel tense, and I have been acting testy. I guess I'm feeling angry because I work hard to make a nice home, and everyone seems careless and unappreciative, and it's a mess in no time. I feel more like Cinderella than the wicked stepmother."

Nondefensive

If self-disclosure is to take place, we must learn not to be defensive. We must learn that feelings, good or bad, right or wrong, must be acknowledged before we can resolve them. But we can't resolve them if we continually defend or justify them.

Take the case in point. Stepmother feels angry and unappreciated. The typical, though not desired, reaction of father and children to the disclosure of her feelings most likely will be, "You shouldn't feel that way." And then they will proceed to tell her why she shouldn't feel that way:

1. "We really do appreciate you"; or
2. "We really aren't as messy as you make us out to be"; and/or
3. "You're too concerned about the appearance of the house."

This kind of response is sure to invite the next salvo from stepmother:

1. "No, you *don't* appreciate me. If you did, you would . . ."; or
2. "What do you mean you're not as messy as I make you out to be?" and/or
3. "What do you mean I'm too concerned about the appearance of the house? This was a pigsty when I moved in!"

Defensiveness—it is destructive to good communication. Rather than be defensive, the stepmother in this case should let things simmer down, and when it's obviously her turn to speak, say, "I have another problem now, which is really bigger than the first one. I tried to be honest about my feelings, but the reaction I got made me feel totally discounted. It seems that my feelings don't matter. I understand that you don't think I should feel as I do. But I'd like my feelings respected, and I'd like us to work on a solution that takes my feelings into account."

By being nondefensive and by respecting the family's point of view, the stepmother avoids an escalation that's bound to go nowhere—accusations and counter-accusations to the point of exhaustion. The attitude is, "This is where I am, for good or bad. I respect my feelings. I don't ask you to agree with me, but I do ask that you respect my feelings as much as your own."

Not Fearful of Positive Attitudes

It may sound strange but we are often afraid of positive attitudes toward others, such as warmth, liking, caring, interest, and respect. The fear comes from two directions. First, we may be disappointed by that person. After all, if you begin to like your stepchild, maybe he won't live up to your expectations. And maybe the child feels the same way. After all, that child has lost one natural parent. Maybe he'll lose you too. It's just too painful to love and lose. Often stepfamilies reflexively keep their guard up.

A second source of fear is that of being trapped—trapped by the expectations of others. If we care about people, they will expect us to show it. But where do you draw the line?

An oft-quoted verse of Scripture is pertinent here. Jesus told us that we are to love our neighbor as ourselves. This is often twisted by the neurotic and the manipulator. The neurotic says, "I should love you instead of myself." The manipulator (children are great at this) reinforces the neurotic's belief and says, "Love me instead of yourself." I don't mean that these words are actually spoken. If they were, we would hear how ridiculous this is. Nevertheless, the attitude prevails.

Take, for example, the sixteen-year-old boy whose stepfather has denied him the use of the family car for the evening. The boy says, "If you were my real father, you wouldn't treat me like this!"

If the stepfather isn't in control of himself, he might say something destructive like, "You first-class ingrate! After everything I've done for you! No, you're right! I'm *not* your real father! But I'll tell you that I've treated you a heck of a lot better than that no-good bum you call a father! If you want a car so bad tonight, call *him* up and see if he'll let you use *his* car!"

Several things probably are going on in the boy's mind when he lashes out at his stepfather. Among them is an idealized view of his real father. This is a tough scene to handle, but the stepfather must handle it. And if he does it right, it will actually strengthen his ability to continue having positive feelings toward his stepson.

The stepfather must realize that he has disappointed stepson's expectations (whether or not those expectations are realistic). But stepfather must realize also that he is not *trapped* by those expectations. Stepfather must remember that caring and love for someone else doesn't mean that you give up caring about *yourself*. If stepson will stay around long enough to hear him, stepfather might say, "I understand that you're disappointed. I just don't feel comfortable about your driving in this snowstorm tonight. I know you have a license and that you'd be careful. But I know myself well enough that my stomach would be in knots until you got home."

What do we have here? Stepson has a need. So does stepfather: he has a need not to have his stomach tied up in knots.

Even if the stepson doesn't stay around long enough to hear what his stepfather has to say, the stepfather can communicate through his attitude, an attitude that says, I love you and respect your needs. But I also love me and respect my needs too. I will try to be fair in meeting your needs and my needs. And when that love is in balance—my love for you and my love for me—then I can love you without fear."

I ask several questions on the Stepparent Test that have a bearing on your ability to do this. Statements 1 and 2 have to do with the quality of patience. Statement 4 has to do with interest and commitment. Questions 6 and 7 have to do with your expecting love and appreciation. The reality is that often you will not feel loved or appreciated. Number 16 should be understood in this context. Stepparenting is not easy. Numbers 21 through 25 all deal with the pressures you will face as a stepparent. You must really want to tackle the job of stepparenting. I realize that children are part of the package deal. But if you can't see yourself learning positive attitudes in the kind of circumstance described above, you had better back off if you're not yet married. If you are, you and the natural parent should have a serious talk about it and maybe even get professional help.

Able to Be a Separate Person

I have already described in some of my illustrations the ability to be a separate person.

We have a strange notion that marriage and the family suddenly make an individual a member of a group. Somehow his *individual* identity, expression, and need becomes *group* identity, expression, and need; and any expression of individuality is heresy. Not true!

Though you are a stepparent and are married to the parent of the stepchild, you have not stopped being an individual. This is important in the natural family but doubly important in the stepfamily where you enter a readymade system. It may be true that the stepchild or stepchildren and parent have their own way of relating. In fact, the history of that system may be of long standing. It is also true that you have been an outsider. But let me shatter the notion right here that you are to become part of *their system*. Though the natural parent and children may have ways of relating that are well established, your entrance into the system *actually creates an entirely new system*. This happens in a natural family every time a child is born. The old system ceases to exist, and a new system is created. Many natural families have problems with additions to the family because they fail to recognize this. They are frustrated because the old system isn't working the way it did. Of course not. It is a new system.

I say this to help stepfamilies understand that their problem is not unique—the disruption of the existing system. Both the natural parent and stepparent can handle this change if they will realize that they should be strong enough as persons to stand separately from the system as well as be part of it. When you are not fearful of losing yourself in the family system, then you can be more accepting and understanding of the stepchild. His depression, fear, and dependence need not engulf you. His anger will not destroy you. Though you are part of this new stepfamily system, you have not lost your separateness as a person.

Able to Grant Others Separateness

The ability to grant others separateness is closely related to the previous issue of being a separate person. Are you able not only to be a separate person yourself but also to grant others their separateness? In helping relationships it is difficult to let the other person be separate and independent from us. This is especially important in helping teen-agers, who by divine providence are given a marvelous ability to be overconfident. If teen-agers knew their real limitations, they'd never grow up and leave home!

The natural family has its share of problems with parents not wanting to let go of the teen-ager. But at least they have the consolation, justified or not, that perhaps the child's training and genetic heritage will save the child when the apron strings are cut.

The stepparent does not have that confidence. In fact, he may be convinced that the child's genetic heritage from the now-absent parent is indeed *defective*. And as far as upbringing is concerned, the child may have developed some bad habits and attitudes long before the stepparent arrived on the scene.

The stepparent must give up the notion that he is going to raise the child "right" and that he must make up for lost time and implement a rigorous program of child training. I'm not sure that I as a natural parent did everything right in raising my children or that they were thoroughly ready to leave home when the time came. Whether or not we're ready or feel that our children are ready, the time for parting ways will come.

I don't think that a stepparent should avoid giving direction or taking a leadership role in the child's life. But when you have done all you can do as a stepparent, you must be able to permit the child not to follow your advice, become independent of you, and mold himself after someone else. As every natural parent knows, this is a gradual process. And just as natural parents have to beware of being supermom or superdad, so stepparents must beware of being superstepmom or dad.

Able to Exercise Accurate Empathy

Accurate empathy is a relational skill that builds on the above. Empathy is a caring attitude that enables us to perceive life the way another person perceives it. It is called *accurate* empathy when we perceive it *exactly* as the other person perceives it. We neither overestimate nor underestimate it. Carl Rogers says,

> *Can I let myself enter fully into the world of his feelings and personal meanings, and see these as he does? Can I step into his private world so completely that I lose all desire to evaluate or judge it? Can I enter it so sensitively that I can move about in it freely, without trampling on meanings which are precious to him? Can I sense it so accurately that I can catch not only the meanings of his experience which are obvious to him, but also those meanings which are only implicit, which he sees only dimly or as confusion? Can I extend this understanding without limit?[2]*

As a stepparent you must be able to do this with your stepchild. Of course, it would be ideal if the child would be sensitive to you as well. But you are the adult. Perhaps by your example the child will learn to practice accurate empathy.

Do you know how torn that child feels—torn with divided loyalties? If he shows you appreciation perhaps he will appear to be disloyal to the absent natural parent. Maybe if he gets too attached to you, you'll leave him too—just as his own parent did. Can you experience his coolness and even ingratitude from his frame of reference? Is the meaning of his world so clear to you that you need not evaluate or judge it? Can you enter so completely into his world that you can say to yourself, "If I were where he is, I'd probably feel that way too"?

I don't mean that accurate empathy should overlook bad behavior. You have needs too. Say, for example, you take your stepson Jeff on a fishing trip with your friends, and all he does is brag about what a great father he has. You feel embarrassed and humiliated in front of your friends.

You have a perfect right to take the boy aside and say, "Jeff, I know that you love your dad and want us to know that he's a great guy. But I really feel embarrassed in front of my friends. It sounds as though I'm not doing a very good job as a stepfather. It's okay to be loyal to your dad. Maybe you could do it in a way that wouldn't make me look bad. I'd really appreciate it."

The boy will probably be defensive and may even accuse you of being a bad stepfather. Unless his accusation is correct, the boy is saying more about himself than you. He's telling you that he's really hurting. At that point he needs understanding more than a lecture.

In the Stepparent Test numbers 9 and 10 should be answered in this light. Effectiveness as a stepparent requires the skill of accurate empathy. Numbers 21 through 25 should be considered here also.

Able to Exercise Nonpossessive Warmth

Nonpossessive warmth is the quality of acceptance of or the ability to show warm feelings toward another person unconditionally. It doesn't mean that you agree with his ideas or approve of his behavior. It does mean that you will care for him because as a human being he is worthy of care. It doesn't mean that you give up your need to protect yourself from his bad behavior. You protect yourself because you care about yourself as much as you care about him. Again, Rogers says,

> Still another issue is whether I can be acceptant of each facet of this other person which he presents to me. Can I receive him as he is? Can I communicate this attitude? Or can I only receive him conditionally, acceptant of some aspects of his feelings and silently or openly disapproving of other aspects? It has been my experience that when my attitude is conditional, then he cannot change or grow in those respects in which I cannot fully receive him.[3]

Stepparents have a difficult time with nonpossessive warmth because too often they come into an existing family system that has a method of operation quite different from what the stepparent is accustomed to. Too often the stepparent takes the attitude, "I'm God's gift to this family. I've arrived in the nick of time to keep you from self-destruction. But I'll get you straightened out." This kind of stepparent makes the natural parent and stepchildren feel like failures. They are insulted, and warfare breaks out immediately!

Numbers 11 through 13 and number 38 on the Stepparent Test should be seen in this light. Many times side-taking and lack of support by the natural parent arise out of a reaction to a lack of nonpossessive warmth. The natural parent feels he or she and the children will be accepted only if they behave as the stepparent thinks they should behave.

Nonthreatening

The quality of being nonthreatening is closely allied to the previous one. Can I relate to the stepchildren and the natural parent with sufficient sensitivity that I'm not perceived as a threat?

A stepparent should not be thought of as an outsider. But if he comes into an existing system with no children of his own, the feeling often does exist. It exists because the system has experienced the trauma of divorce. There has been a lot of hurt. A parent and spouse has left. Though the stepchildren and their parent are hopeful that this new stepfamily will offer a fulfilling experience, maybe you as the stepparent can't be trusted fully by either the stepchild or the parent. Can you enter their world in a nonthreatening manner?

Maybe the stepchildren view you as a threat even though you're not. Can you accept the fact that even though *you* don't see yourself as a threat, the children might? Can you respect that feeling and act with sensitivity?

Don't make the mistake of putting the burden on the child with the attitude, "I'm no threat, and if you feel I am, that's *your* problem." Try to make it your problem too. I don't mean making it your problem to the point that the child strips you of all authority as a stepparent and manipulates you with it. The child should know that you understand and accept the fact that he sees you as a threat, and that's okay. You will attempt to be sensitive to his feelings, short of being manipulated. And you will attempt to enter his life in a nonthreatening way.

Numbers 12 through 14 on the Stepparent Test should be considered in light of this. Often, side-taking and favoritism are reactions to a perceived threat.

Nonjudgmental

Nonthreatening people tend to be nonjudgmental. This doesn't mean that you don't have your own ideas about how a successful stepfamily should function. It doesn't mean that you give up exercising what you feel is good judgment. It means that you resist the temptation to evaluate the other person's performance in a negative light.

A judgmental attitude often comes through in subtle ways. Sometimes it comes through in statements such as—

- *"My* way of doing it is . . ."; or
- "Well, if you had a little more common sense, you would . . ."; or
- "I'd never let *my* kids. . . ."

If you already feel as though you're an outsider, this kind of talk is bound to keep you there.

In my book *Just Talk to Me* I deal with this in my discussion of roadblocks to good communication. The entire chapter on acceptance also deals with this issue.

We need to be aware that we may also be guilty of judging with a positive evaluation as well. When we inform someone that he is good, it implies the right to tell him when he is bad too. Please understand that I believe Christian parents should teach their children the difference beween right and wrong. "Good" and "bad" are proper moral distinctions. But too often parents and stepparents confuse performance with moral correctness. A child may be morally good when honest and morally bad when he lies, cheats, or steals. He is not bad, however, when he does a sloppy job of cutting the grass. He is not good when he does a thorough job of shoveling the snow. His moral goodness is not totally dependent on his performance.

Christian parents often wonder why their children have a difficult time with the concept of grace—that we are unconditionally accepted by God through faith in Christ our Savior. Children tend to hang on to the notion that acceptance by God depends on their *performance*. Yet the same parents turn around and give the child the message that *parental* acceptance *does* depend on performance.

I have one son left at home. He is accepted unconditionally because he is my son. This doesn't mean that his performance is unimportant—that he can behave as he wishes. As much as it lies within my control, I will have something to say about his performance. But his performance stands quite apart from his position as my son and my acceptance of him as my son. I want our relationship to be exactly as my relationship is to God. I give my Father my best performance not *to be* accepted but because I am already unconditionally accepted as a member of His family. And, in fact, being a member of that family is such a privilege, I would be ashamed to turn in less than my best performance! The sacred author had it right—both in the family of God and man—when he wrote that we love the Father because He first loved us (1 John 4:19).

Open to Change

The final quality of a helpful stepparent is the openness to change. This quality is important to the natural parent as well as to the stepparent. Both bring into the new system their own ideas of what good parenting is all about. In the case of the natural family many times the parents are able to sort out their differences before the child is old enough to know that they have had their disagreements over how to raise the child. But frequently this does not happen. Their disagreements over how to raise the child go on and on until the child is old enough to understand the situation and exploit it with divide-and-conquer tactics.

In the stepfamily the stepparent enters a system where the

natural parent and child already have established certain ground rules for the parent-child relationship. The rigid stepparent who thinks the natural parent is going about the job all wrong is in big trouble. The stepparent may have his or her own opinion, but he or she should be open to change.

Fred married Alice, who brought two daughters into the marriage. Fred thought that Alice let the girls get away with too much; and after months of heated arguments, he decided that he would let Alice handle the girls and that he would have nothing to do with discipline or direction. It was true that Alice needed to tighten up on the girls' behavior. But Fred was complicating things. He was so rigid and closed to the idea of doing anything different from the way he thought it should be done, he actually created more opposition to his way. This wound up in a stalemate and eventually a divorce. This is why children are a major cause of failure for second marriages. The stepparent and the existing system must be open to change.

Summary

Most of what I've discussed here has to do with communication. Remarried couples who are having trouble communicating and applying these principles should read my book *Just Talk to Me*. It is written to help couples communicate. And when you learn to communicate effectively with each other, you will be able to do it with your children and stepchildren as well.

7.

Stepmother: Wicked Witch or Wonder Woman?

Let's sharpen our focus a little more. In the last chapter we considered some general principles that stepmothers and stepfathers both must apply to their relations with their stepchildren. Now let us consider some special concerns of stepmothers.

The Stepmother's Wants

Ruth Roosevelt and Jeannette Lofas, who are both stepmothers themselves, have written a book entitled *Living in Step*. It's about stepfamilies, and they include an entire chapter about the stepmother's wants.[1] They say that her desire for recognition seems to be a major one, and the lack of it one of her deepest dissatisfactions. This need comes from several directions.

Recognition From the Children's Natural Mother. The stepmother needs recognition from the natural mother; and she resents it when the natural mother doesn't seem to appreciate how hard she is trying to meet her children's needs and make them happy.

Emotional Support From the Children's Father. The children's father also needs to appreciate and support her emotionally. After all, she's giving so much for *his* children—at least this is her feeling. Though she should not use the children to get closer to their dad (see Stepparent Test number 26), she needs to know that he appreciates her and supports her in her work.

Appreciation From the Stepchildren. Even though she should not *expect* love and appreciation from her stepchildren, the stepmother certainly does want it. Does she feel that the stepchildren take her for granted? Does she feel appreciated by them? Or is there a feeling of unappreciation, aggravated by the children's thoughtless comments, such as, "Mom's _____ is better"—whether this refers to mom's cooking or something else. The children often don't realize how hard they are trying to be loyal to their natural mother, but even knowing this herself doesn't always help the stepmother hurt less. Numbers 6 and 7 on the Stepparent Test should be discussed in light of this.

Wanting to Come First. Is the stepmother's relationship with her husband the primary relationship? Or does she always feel left out? Sometimes matters are made worse by the natural competition a teen-age stepdaughter offers her. Daughters naturally compete with their mothers or stepmothers for the attention and affection of their fathers. This is their way of validating their femininity and testing their emerging social skills.

Mothers often find this difficult to handle. Stepmothers find it intolerable. As one stepmother said to me. "Bill's daughter will tease him and act playful—poking and tickling him in a way that I don't like. It's like the kind of thing you see a girl do to her boyfriend. *I don't like it!*"

Several items on the Stepparent Test touch on this. They need to be discussed in this light. They are numbers 12, 14, 15, 19, 27, 35, 36, and 40.

A Child of Her Own. Sometimes because the stepmother never had a child of her own, she wants one now. Often, the husband does not want one because he has had his family and is older than she.

The National Vital Statistics System shows that single women who marry divorced men are on the average six years younger. Single women who marry widowed men are on an average fourteen years younger.

This may be an important issue for the stepmother with no children of her own. This is why I included item number 8 on the Stepparent Test.

Dealing With the "Other Woman." The children will always be a link with her husband's former wife, while the stepmother needs to feel that the door is closed on that relationship.

Even though her husband may have no affection for his former wife, his concern for her may anger his new wife. She may feel that she doesn't get the consideration his former wife gets! Or she may feel that the former wife is an intrusive force. She may resent this intrusion into the stepfamily and have no way to cope with it. The Stepparent Test considers this and related concerns in numbers 11, 34, 35, and 41.

As I survey the literature on the subject of stepparenting, particularly the image and role of the stepmother, I am uneasy because it appears that she is the victim of two hoaxes. One hoax is that we *say* we don't believe in the wicked stepmother myth any longer, but the myth is alive and well. The other hoax is that we are all "enlightened" people now. We are supposed to have egalitarian families, both natural and step. The husband and wife are equal, so it goes. This equality, it is said, is seen in the fact that they are both breadwinners, they share household chores, and together they raise the children.

I say that these are hoaxes. The wicked stepmother myth continues. And the family is not egalitarian. The husband usually earns more money and is considered the primary breadwinner. The wife, though she may work outside the home and may have her husband's help at home, is still the "primary" parent—she is responsible for homemaking and the children. Let me support these assertions.

Living Down the Image

Stepmothers have been maligned in fairy tales for centuries. Hansel and Gretel were twice abandoned by their stepmother in the forest. Snow White's stepmother out of jealousy tried to poison her. Cinderella's stepmother made her the household servant while the natural daughters were permitted an indulgent life.

The Basis of the Mythology. Why is it that stepmothers got such bad press and stepfathers didn't? There is a historical reason, and it's not because stepfathers are nicer people.

These fairy tales were written at a time when divorce was almost unheard of. There simply were not a lot of divorced men becoming the stepfathers of other men's children.

It was also a time that was hard on women—they often died in childbirth or died young of other causes, leaving a father with children and no mother to take care of them. Because of the high mortality rate, it was not unusual for a man to have several wives successively. No wonder divorce wasn't such a problem in those days. The mortality rate saw to that!

Someone is sure to say, "You don't really believe that stepmothers labor under this mythology today, do you?" Yes, I do.

Consider Lois, who has been the stepmother of two children for six years. She says, "I don't like being called a stepmother! For instance, when I take the kids for shots or if they get hurt, when I say I'm their adopted mother I'm treated in a different way, as though I really want them and am trying to help them. But when I say I'm a stepmother, it's like 'she did this to the kid.' I resent this."[2]

It is hoped that time will reverse this myth. This letter from a stepchild is encouraging:

> So often when the word "stepparent" comes up in a conversation, people go right to Cinderella and say, "Oh, poor child." Boy, are they mixed up!
>
> My parents were divorced when I was seven. I am now sixteen, and both parents have remarried. I live with my mother and visit my dad in the summer and on some school vacations. My relationship with my stepmother is a beautiful one. We can, and have, talked about everything possible. She is one of my best friends in the world. My stepfather hasn't been around very long, but we are getting along better and better all the time.
>
> Of course, it takes some work. Sharing. I had to get used to sharing my mom and dad, and at first it is tough to take orders. You have to remember, though, that they're going through heck trying to be accepted by you.
>
> I have learned and grown very much from having stepparents. Evil Stepmother?! It was probably Cinderella's fault![3]

I'm encouraged by this letter, but feel uneasy at the same time. It sounds *too* good.

This Is My Stepmother. My mother died in 1967. I was a pastor in Arlington, Virginia, at the time, and I officiated at her funeral.

Six months later I accepted a call to a church in Southern California, and dad moved to the coast with us. It wasn't long before he met a lovely woman, Idalee, in the church and married her. I had the privilege of officiating at the wedding. I tease my father about it—it's not every son who gets to officiate at his own father's wedding.

Even as I write this I am full of emotion—the bittersweet memories of burying my mother and marrying my father. Pop and Idalee are happy, and I'm happy for them. He needs Idalee at this time of his life. But I wasn't prepared for my reaction to having a stepmother. What would I call her? "Mother" is inappropriate because she's not my mother. I would feel disloyal to the memory of my mother if I called her that. "Stepmother" would sound like an insult, considering the mythology that goes along with the name. I finally settled on "Idalee," though I'm not completely satisfied with that either. She is my father's wife and ought to be given the recognition due her position.

For a long time I couldn't even address my letters to them as Mr. and Mrs. Raymond A. Bustanoby. I addressed them to Ray and Idalee Bustanoby. Then I realized that this was an insult to Idalee. She *is* Mrs. Raymond A. Bustanoby. She is giving my father a full and happy life, and she loves him dearly. How dare I take away from her the right to that title! I was treating her as a second-class citizen! Perhaps the myth of the wicked stepmother is still alive!

But this conflict of loyalty between my dead mother and stepmother continued. Once it surfaced inadvertently in public. I was conducting a workshop on communication at a Christian Booksellers Convention in Anaheim, California. Pop and Idalee came to the workshop, and I publicly acknowledged their presence. I introduced them as "my father, Ray Bustanoby, and Idalee."

It wasn't until later that I realized how that might have sounded to the people at the workshop. The gentleman whom I introduced was obviously my father, but who was this Idalee? A friend of the family? A distant relative?

There I was—a fifty-one-year-old man with a good education, years of experience as a pastor and marriage-and-family therapist, and I didn't know how to introduce my own stepmother! The mythology of the wicked stepmother is so pervasive and culturally entangled, I found I didn't know how to relate to a stepmother whom I dearly love and to whom I am grateful, from the bottom of my heart, for giving my dad a good life! If there is *dignity* to being a stepmother, why can't I utter the word without feeling that I've hurled an insult?

The Wonder Woman. I believe that the old mythology has given rise to a new mythology as a reaction. It is the myth that a good stepmother has to be a Wonder Woman. She has to be Superstepmother!

I do not believe that stepfathers face nearly as much pressure to perform well as stepmothers do. And though it hurts a stepfather not to be appreciated by his stepchildren, I believe that the stepmother runs the risk of greater hurt, especially when she has tried to live down the wicked-stepmother myth by being Superstepmother.

But there is another danger in trying too hard. Family therapists find this frequently in natural families. And it is usually the mother rather than the father who is to blame for trying too hard.

Trying too hard, whether in the natural or stepfamily, sets up the mother or stepmother for failure. She then suffers secondary symptoms of low self-worth and anger at her children and sometimes her husband. If it persists, it leads to a physical and emotional breakdown. The stepmother is especially vulnerable to trying too hard because she has this unfair myth to live down. She must prove to her darling, adorable stepchildren that she's not the wicked stepmother of fairy-tale fame!

Stepmother, listen to me. Whenever you put yourself in a situation with children where you must *prove* yourself, you're in trouble—big trouble. You set yourself up for a manipulation that children are masters at. It works like this.

You try hard to be nice and to please your stepchildren. In fact, your meals, the appearance of the house, your willingness to chauffeur them and do whatever they want—your total performance is almost flawless. But what happens? They can't afford to admit that you're doing a good job. That would take away their opportunity to get even more from you. The name of the game is to critically appraise your performance, in both word and attitude, and to give you the message, "You're doing pretty well for a stepmother. But if you *really* want to improve your performance then you will—

- Iron my skirt, right now;
- Put a patch on my jeans, right now;
- Not hassle me about chores;
- Take me over to Jack's house, right now;
- Give me five dollars for lunch. . . ."

The list is limited only by the imagination and desires of the children.

Of course the implication behind these demands is, "If you don't do this, we will all know that the fairy tales are true. Stepmothers *are* wicked!" And of course this is followed with, "Because you're so rotten, we can be just as uncooperative as we want!" Certainly this is extreme. But it does happen in various ways.

Stepmothers should also be aware of an opposite reaction, however. It's an anxiety reaction in the child that comes out of a feeling of insecurity. You have entered a family situation where, because of a divorce, the child has become alert to anything that might suggest things are not well. As he watches you try so hard, he wonders about it. From his experience, most parents don't try that hard. He starts to feel insecure and wonders what's wrong: "Are stepmother and father not getting along? Is the job of being a stepmother too much for her? Will it push her off the deep end? Maybe that's why mom left. It's tough being a mother or stepmother. Will she leave too? Boy, I'd better behave myself. What can I do to keep her from leaving too?" The result is something called "the too-good child" who winds up with somatic reactions. This is why I was uneasy about the letter from the sixteen-year-old girl quoted earlier. She could become a "too-good child" very easily.

What's a stepmother to do? Stop trying so hard. In word and attitude you must give a clear message to your family, father and children alike—and if you bring your own children into the marriage, let them hear it too. The message is this: "I want you all to know that I'm not a wicked witch or Wonder Woman. There will be times when I please you and times when I disappoint you. That's just an occupational hazard that I have to put up with and that you'll have to put up with too. I'm not a replacement for the stepchildren's mother. I'm just a normal human being who's going to do the best I can. Though I will listen to your wants, wishes, and criticisms, *I* will make the final judgment on my performance. And if my best is not good enough, I'm sorry."

Your attitude should be calm and matter-of-fact—an attitude that says, "I'm doing the best I can. And that's good enough."

The Role of the Stepmother

At the beginning of this chapter I said that the stepmother is the victim of two cruel hoaxes. The second hoax is that today we believe in egalitarianism, that husbands and wives are equals in the American stepfamily. In spite of all the talk about husbands sharing equally the parenting and homemaking responsibilities with the stepmother, I don't see it happening. They do share, but by no means is there equal sense of responsibility.

I am not against role differentiation. In fact I believe that clear husband-and-wife roles help a family run smoothly and efficiently. What I object to is the nonsense that husbands and wives feel equally responsible for all phases of family life, that we have come to an equitable division of responsibilities, and that there are no role distinctions in the modern American stepfamily. This simply is not true.

Stepmother As "Primary" Parent. The American family today, whether natural or step, is far more traditional than most people like to admit. And this is understandable because we have not established a new role model for a stepmother.

A recent study called "The Role of the Stepmother" concluded that

the step-mother's role today is less clear than in the past. Women becoming step-mothers, with and without natural children, are in a role that is not only ill-defined, but one that is further complicated by the folklore portrayed of the "wicked step-mother" or the expectation of "instant motherly love" toward the step-children. Either or both of these social and psychological implications has made the role of step-mother misunderstood, difficult and unrewarding.[4]

The study did point out that the role of the stepmother without natural children tended to differ from that of the mother with natural chidren. The stepmother without natural children tended to have a greater provider role. But interestingly, there was not significant difference between the two in her role as homemaker, organizer, and participant in recreational activities. And this brings me to the very point I want to make.

In the absence of a new role model for the stepmother, I believe we have turned to the traditional model of the mother in the American home, a model which I describe as "mother, the 'primary' parent." By "primary" I mean that she is given, *and she accepts,* the responsibility for the organization and administration of the household and supervision of the children. I don't mean that the husband fails to help, but there seems to be an unspoken agreement that the organization and administration of the home and supervision of the children is her primary responsibility.

Roles also tend to be traditional when it comes to the husband. Though the wife may work a full-time job outside the home and her income is probably necessary, the unspoken agreement is that the husband is the primary provider.

If you don't believe that the mother or stepmother is the primary parent, think for a minute:

1. Who is responsible to see that the children receive inoculations, medical care when ill, and dental care and that they are chauffuered to the doctor and dentist?

2. Who is responsible for keeping track of the schedule of sports practices, games, lessons, and social activities and to see that the children are chauffuered or have transportation?

3. Who is responsible for the menu, meal planning, grocery shopping, and preparation of meals? It is true that husbands are taking more responsibility along this line. But who has the ultimate responsibility to see that it is done?

4. Who is responsible for getting the clothes washed and ironed? More and more men are helping with the laundry, but who has the ultimate responsibility? I know few men who know how to iron a daughter's frilly white blouse, let alone teach her how to do it. Can you imagine a stepdaughter saying to her stepfather, "I'm in a terrible rush to get off to my date. Would you mind ironing my blouse while I take my shower?"

5. Who is responsible for keeping track of the children, whom they're with, what they're doing, and how they're behaving? Father may back up stepmother, cooperate, and even take the initiative in critical matters. But the daily routine generally falls on her.

6. When the children are sick, who stays home from work or makes special arrangements for their care? Usually mother or stepmother. I know of some cases where stepmother was away on a business trip or had an important business meeting to attend and father stayed home. But when he did, the feeling was that *he* had to bail *her* out; she couldn't do her stepmotherly job at home, so he had to. And he made it clear that it better not happen too often because he might lose his job. And since he earns more money than she, his job takes priority!

I am not trying to be hard on the husband. I'm just asking that we stop perpetrating the hoax of the egalitarian marriage and family. There is nothing wrong with the mother or stepmother's being the "primary" parent. But we should be honest about it and be clear about our role expectations.

Let me suggest that you sharpen your focus on role expectations by playing "The Buck Stops Here." Let's say that something important has to be done, but it's not done. Who takes the responsibility for it's not being done? For example, ten-year-old Johnny is the star forward of his soccer team. He has an important practice Saturday at 7:00 A.M. Who takes the initiative to see that he has transportation? Dad or stepmother? The answer to this kind of question will help you sort out role expectations. You will probably learn that the stepmother is indeed the primary parent and is ultimately responsible for the organization and administration of the home and the supervision of the children.

Stepmother As Friend. Another finding of the study previously referred to, "The Role of the Stepmother," found that the majority of stepmothers selected the role of friend, rather than attempting to replace the natural mother or trying to be an additional mother figure.

It is wise not to try to replace mother. In fact, the stepmother's attitude should be, "I'm not going to replace your mother. You already have one." But I don't feel comfortable with the idea of her being a "friend" in contradistinction to "mother figure." The stepmother and children are not peers or equals. They are not nor will they ever be—nor should they be.

You may ask, "If not friend, mother, or mother figure, what then is a stepmother?" You can understand why one confused stepmother defined herself as a bird that sits on another bird's eggs. The stepmother who said that probably is as confused as you are about what a stepmother is. Society is at a loss for an adequate modern definition.

Rather than stating a definition of a stepmother, let me suggest a description. *A stepmother is the significant, resident female adult in the stepfamily and the wife and peer of the natural father.* I could enlarge on this description by saying that although she is not a replacement for the mother, she has a responsibility to cooperate with the father in maintaining the order and discipline of the family. As significant, resident female adult, she is accorded in the home the same respect and privilege due her position that other significant female adults have in the lives of the children. I have in mind schoolteachers, principals, and law enforcement officials. As resident female adult in the home and wife of the children's father, she is to provide a role model for the children as female guide of the children's welfare in family life and organizer and administrator of the home. This assumes, of course, that she accepts the role of "primary" parent. As wife of the children's father, she models a successful adult relationship with an adult male in marriage and demonstrates how a husband and wife can effectively cooperate in raising children, whether they are natural or stepchildren.

It is all right for a stepmother to think of herself as the stepchildren's friend so long as she sees herself in the role of significant, resident female adult who is the wife and peer of the children's father. The reason why I include that last part of the description is that she must be a friend from the position of strength and dignity. In other settings, such as school or summer camp, adults become friends with children out of such a position. In any organization—whether home, school, or summer camp—the ultimate question is, "Who is in charge here, and who has the legal responsibility for these children?" You had better be ready to answer, "Their father and I are responsible. I am the custodial stepmother of these children." I will be dealing with this issue further in my discussion of stepchildren, but in every family the question of who's in charge is important.

It may sound contemporary for a child to say, "My friend here is in charge." But when it comes down to physical and emotional welfare or life-and-death issues, "my friend here" (the stepmother) should have more than likeability. She should exhibit maturity, common sense, and a sense of responsibility. I believe that people who are in charge should exude competency.

Stepmother, whether you like it or not, you are in charge. Of course, the responsibility is shared with the children's father. No, you won't replace the children's mother. No, you're not just their friend. You might even resemble a mother-figure. The fact is, there's really no adequate name or description for you. And maybe that's good. It gives you the freedom to be *you* with all the gifts that God has given you. As you play out your role of stepmother as only you can, you will draw on your past family life and God-honored traditions and help formulate a model for the stepmother of the future.

Don't be afraid of the traditional role of "primary" parent if this is what you are comfortable with. That is the key—you must feel comfortable with your role, and this must be clearly understood from the beginning. Don't be conned by talk of egalitarian marriage. If stepmother really is the primary parent and father is the primary provider, then let's say so.

You live in an exciting time of social development where the mythology of the wicked stepmother is slowly dying. Don't try to replace it with a new mythology—that of the Wonder Woman, Super-stepmother. Relax and be yourself with all the talent and limitations God has given you. And in the process help develop a new tradition of American stepmotherhood.

8.

What to Expect of a Stepfather

Stepfathers, like stepmothers, have special concerns and needs in the stepfamily. Many of the stepfathers' concerns are the same as the stepmothers'.

Curt Gallenkamp, noted Indiana psychologist, gives seven pointers to men who are marrying women with children. He says that the stepfather should—

1. *Acquire as much awareness as possible of what he is getting into. This awareness includes knowledge of the woman and her feelings but also of his own feelings and the feelings of the children.*
2. *Get as much history on the "new" family as possible.*
3. *Resolve the authority-control issue as quickly as possible. No matter what the situation, it's highly unlikely that the stepfather will have control over his stepchildren in the beginning.*
4. *Develop love and an adequate, positive communication/listening system between husband and wife.*
5. *Understand that the stepchildren need love . . . even though they may not ask for it in the beginning.*
6. *Not get hurt or feel rejected too quickly. . . .*
7. *Seek out pre-marital, stepparent counseling. . . .*[1]

Dr. Gallenkamp is quite right in offering this advice. But these are not uniquely stepfather concerns. Stepmothers are concerned about more of the same issues.

However, one issue mentioned by Dr. Gallenkamp is uniquely

a stepfather concern. It is number 3, the authority-control issue. My survey of literature on stepfathering reveals this to be a primary concern again and again. The stepfather is put into the position of father figure, one who is supposed to exercise authority and control, but who often feels thwarted in his attempt to fill that role.

Another unique concern surfaced in my research. Though it is true that both the stepmother and stepfather have a strong need to be appreciated by the stepchildren, each has his or her own special area of need. The stepmother needs appreciation in her role as homemaker and primary caretaker of the children. The stepfather has a need to be appreciated for his financial support of the children.

I am not saying that the stepmother never wants to be appreciated for her financial contribution to the family. In fact, I include items on the Stepparent Test that address this very issue. Numbers 32 through 35 deal with the resentments the stepmother has over money. However, each has a basic area of responsibility, and each would like to see some appreciation for fulfilling that responsibility.

Authority and Control

Roosevelt and Lofas are right when they say that the stepmother operates against omnipresent myths of cruelty. However, the stepfather operates against an absence of myth, an unspoken assumption that his role is to play no role.[2] Let me carry this one step further. Having no clearly defined historical role, the stepfather tends to revert to the traditional father role, "male head of the household." And yet he is often thwarted in filling that role. In my counseling I often perceive that the natural mother likes the feeling of security that comes with the idea of a male head of the household, but she wants none of the liabilities. By this I mean that if the man is going to be put in the position of having authority over and control of the woman's child, she cannot veto every move he makes in his attempt to fill that role. When this happens, it's not long before the family plunges toward destruction in a deadly tailspin. Consider the following:

- Stepfather disciplines stepchild.
- Stepchild complains to mother.
- Mother defends child and becomes angry at stepfather.
- Stepfather retreats from stepchild in self-defense.
- Stepmother complains that stepfather will have nothing to do with stepchild.
- Stepfather attempts to resume relations with child, including discipline, but is wrong again—and the cycle starts all over.

Stepfather Without Authority. This was Michael's complaint. He was the stepfather of a son and daughter and the noncustodial parent of his own son and daughter. Though both sets of children were approximately the same ages, he showed more interest in his own children than his stepchildren.

Rita, his wife, complained bitterly about this and felt insecure about the amount of time Michael spent with his former wife discussing the needs of his children. "The least he can do," said Rita, "is give my children and me equal time."

"How can I?" asked Michael. "Every time I try to give my input and say how I feel things should be done, I get the distinct message from Rita, 'That's not the way we do it around here.' And I get looks from her kids that say, 'Mom's right. That's not how we do it around here.' Sure, I show more interest in my own kids. They're willing to listen to me. And my ex gives me far more latitude with my kids than I have with Rita's. I know that Rita helps support the family, but sometimes I feel the only thing I'm good for around here is a meal ticket."

Michael was bitter. "If Rita wants to run the house and the kids, fine. But she has no right to expect me to exercise any authority or control over her kids when it's her show. I can't give her and her kids equal time. She won't let me. Maybe when the kids are grown up and gone, we can make a life of our own. We get along great when it's just the two of us. But the moment the kids enter the picture, Rita becomes a different woman. I'm not going to fight her for the right to—" Michael hesitated. Then he continued, "I don't even *know* what I'm supposed to be doing. This is why I'm either with my own kids or at the office. At least I know what I'm supposed to be doing *there*."

The Stepfather Role. I have said that the absence of a clear stepfather role encourages the tendency toward a traditional father role—that of authority and control. I don't mean that mother has no control or authority. It is a shared responsibility. Father, working in concert with mother, serves as a backup when her authority is challenged; and if the challenge is severe, father has sufficient clout to stop a child who is out of control. Does this sound terribly out of touch with the times?

I believe that we have failed our children and stepchildren because we have not exercised "tough love." By this I don't mean physical abuse. What I mean is that a father or stepfather who loves and understands children has a responsibility to use his size, strength, knowledge of the law, and a mature application of it to bring the child under control. A child is truly free when he is under control.

Parents and stepparents have a responsibility to set boundaries around the child. Once the child understands those boundaries, he should be given freedom to grow within them. A stepfather working with the children's mother can help the mother control and mold the children into responsible adults who understand boundaries and limits. But he must be given the freedom to do so.

I realize some stepfathers are cruel and abusive. And often the children's mother feels caught in a bind between wanting the stepfather to be an active authority, yet not exposing her children to humiliation and physical abuse. Any stepmother who has this problem should get professional help. The system is self-destructive and requires outside intervention.

More frequent is the problem where the stepfather backs off from confrontation. He feels that his role is ambiguous; or worse, he feels as though he is an intruder into "their" family, the family of the wife and stepchildren.

What then *is* the role of the stepfather? He is a "father figure," but different from the biological father. He is not a replacement for the father. What then? I describe him as I do the stepmother. He is the significant adult male head of the household and the husband of the children's mother.

The idea of a stepparent's having authority over a stepchild is not strange. Every day adults, who are not the child's parents, have authority—beginning with the schoolbus driver who takes the child to school. Mothers need to be careful that they are not so protective of their children that they fail to permit other significant adults to have a place of authority and control in their children's lives.

One more thing about the stepfather role. In describing the stepfather I include the statement that he is "the husband of the children's mother." I do so with Jack and Karen in mind.

Jack and Karen came for counseling with a classic problem. Jack felt as though he was an intruder in "Karen's family," which is made up of Karen and her twin daughters, Linda and Laura.

"Karen says she wants me to be an active part of the family," began Jack, "but I have no freedom to give any point of view about the way things are done or to do things my way. It always has to be Karen's way."

Karen raised her eyebrows and replied defensively, "Well, *they* are *my* children!"

Jack shot back, "Well, *you* are *my wife!*"

"What's that supposed to mean?"

"I mean that when we married, we became one. We decided to make a life together. And we've done pretty well. We have one bank account and one budget. We both behave ourselves in our relations to the opposite sex and feel secure with each other. We don't cut each other down in front of our friends. You're always considerate of how I think and feel except in one area—the kids.

"The moment the subject of the kids comes up, it's like you pull down a shade over your face. It's as though you're saying to me, 'This is a closed area of my life. As far as the kids are concerned, you're an outsider.'

"How can I feel close to you, at one with you, when there's a big part of your life that you won't share with me?"

Karen responded defensively, "What do you mean, I won't share this part of my life with you? I'm always asking you to take an active part with the girls, as any father would. They don't always listen to me, and I can't keep my eye on them all the time to make sure they're doing what they should."

"You're right." Jack sighed, lowered his voice and said in

even, quiet tones. "You *do* ask me to become a more active parent; but the moment I do, you become an entirely different person. You are the most understanding, warmest person I know when we're on any subject but the kids. I'm heard and understood, and that makes me feel good—as though I'm a part of you. You respect my judgment and opinions as well as your own. We come up with great solutions that are based on mutual respect for each other's feelings—on everything but the kids.

"When we talk about the kids, your face clouds up, your voice becomes tense and testy, and *nothing,* I mean nothing, I say means anything. Yes, Karen, the message is loud and clear. They are *your children.*

"But I say to myself, 'I am *her husband.*' Doesn't that mean anything to you? And what hurts me most is that I think the children pick up your message of distrust in my ability to be a good stepfather. I think they see *you* doubt my ability, so *they* doubt my ability. Karen, in every other relationship we have with people, you're my biggest fan. But with your kids, at best I'm an intruder; at worst, an ogre."

As I listened to Jack and Karen, I began to see that it was Karen's guilt that created this situation. She felt that her children had been hurt badly by the previous marriage and divorce, and she was determined to protect them from any more hurt. Out of her feeling of guilt, she refused to make her relationship with Jack the primary relationship.

In reality the girls were not damaged, but their mother's strong defensive posture started to make them feel that perhaps they had been damaged and that they should be afraid of further damage. Not only was Karen ruining her marriage, she was also turning the twins into neurotics. After all, if mother was so concerned about their welfare, maybe there really was something· to be afraid of. And if mother didn't trust Jack's judgment, then the girls ought not to trust it either.

Karen eventually came to see that her attitude toward Jack as stepfather was crucial to her children's attitude. By changing her attitude and saying by it, "This is my husband whom I love and trust," Karen was able to let the girls know that Jack had a place in the system too. Yes, they were her daughters and as such had an important place in her life. But Jack was her husband and *he* had an important place in her life too. And part of his place in her life was to share her children and the responsibility of them with her.

As Karen showed confidence in Jack's ability to be a good stepfather and believed that he had the girls' welfare at heart, she encouraged the girls to feel the same way. I believe that no matter how good a stepfather might be, *the children's mother has the power to make or break him.*

Several items on the Stepparent Test relate to this problem. You may find it helpful to review and talk about them in light of this discussion. See especially the following: 1, 3, 9, 12, 14, 19, 20, 27, 37, 38, 41.

Money and Support

Two big spoilers in stepfamilies are problems with the stepchildren and problems with money. With money I include the general subject of support, which involves alimony and/or child support, the time the stepfather spends with his own noncustodial children, whom he includes in his will, and how he handles the question of adopting his stepchildren.

The Overwhelmed Stepfather. On the Stepparent Test number 31 addresses this issue—the stepfather who feels overwhelmed at having to support two families. This is often complicated by the wife who resents support payments to the other family (see test no. 33) and often has to work to help support her own family because of it (see no. 32).

Get the picture? Here is a man barely making it financially, supporting his stepfamily and natural family. Life is joyless. Add to this a wife who is unhappy about this drain on the family resources and feels resentful at having to work outside the home. As though that's not lethal enough, add to the explosive brew the fact that the man doesn't feel appreciated for his hard work by either family. His natural family and stepfamily both take him for granted. Add to this the stepchildren, who respect neither his possessions nor living space—he always feels crowded by them (see test nos. 42 and 43). Mix all of this thoroughly and set it off with a jealous wife who says, "You're always doing more for your ex-wife and her kids than for me and my kids" (see test no. 34).

I have seen this lethal combination blow apart several step-families. In one case the stepfather had to be hospitalized for a physical and emotional breakdown. He was diagnosed as schizophrenic, but I believe that he was getting even. Neither his natural family nor stepfamily seemed to appreciate his heroic efforts at taking care of them. Now they could take care of *him*.

A tragedy like this can be averted if the husband will talk about his feelings constructively, using a nonattacking "I" message. He needs to say to his wife, "Honey, I feel overwhelmed by the demands of two families. Life is grim and a drudgery. And sometimes I feel worse when I think that you resent my child-support payments and your having to work to keep us afloat. I feel inadequate and guilty for putting this on you.

"I know you often feel taken for granted. I do too. And not only that, I get angry when it seems that the kids are destructive and crowd my need for space.

"But the biggest guilt trip for me is when I hear that I'm doing more for my former wife and my kids than I do for you and yours. I love you, and I hurt when I think that you feel that you're coming up on the short end."

This kind of communication follows two basic principles:

1. When you communicate, it is to achieve *understanding* not *agreement*. You may not convince each other of what is right, but you will at least understand each other. If you can achieve this, a mutually satisfactory solution is not far away. You're open to finding one that you both can live with.

2. Constructive communication is nonattacking and nondefensive.

The Stepfather's Will. Immediate support is not the only issue stepfathers must consider. Long-term support is also important, particularly in view of the fact that the stepfather could die before either the natural children or stepchildren become self-supporting. What about his will?

It may be helpful to see the stepfather as having primary and secondary responsibilities. His primary responsibility is to his current wife and his children, whether or not his children live with him. His secondary responsibility is to the former wife and his stepchildren, if his stepchildren live with him (see test no. 33).

1. Primary responsibility. When the man divorced and remarried, he dissolved one legal responsibility and assumed a new one. The terms of the divorce property settlement spell out the limits of any legal claim his former wife has. Apart from those claims, the former wife is on her own to fend for herself. This might sound unfeeling, but this is the way it must be if the new marriage is to survive. The new marriage is the man's primary responsibility apart from the claims of the former spouse or the children. If this is so, the man's will must provide for the support of his current wife if he should die. What about his former wife? Her claims were to have been settled at the time of divorce.

I also name *his* children as a "primary responsibility," and I make a distinction between "primary relationship" and "primary responsibility." His children should not intrude into his *relationship* with his new wife. The husband-wife *relationship* is primary. But the father is still responsible for the support of his children. He may divorce his wife and settle her claims in court, but he can't divorce his children. They will always be his children.

The will should reflect the primary nature of these responsibilities. How the father chooses to do this is a matter of his own judgment and legal counsel. But it should be done in a manner that reflects his care for his new wife and his children. The new wife must not feel that her husband's loyalties, as reflected in his will, are slanted wholly toward his children. This can poison a marriage.

I think that the agreement should provide adequately for his current wife in the event of his death. His children should receive what they would have received from his estate if he had not divorced. It is likely that his estate will be modest, so he should consider some kind of insurance plan. But he should be careful what kind he purchases.[3]

2. Secondary responsibility. The stepfather's secondary responsibility is his former wife and his stepchildren who are living with him. It would be nice if he could be generous to everyone, but his resources are limited.

The property settlement should have closed out the claims his former wife had. If he dies and leaves behind minor children in her custody, the children should be taken care of out of his estate. However, it becomes a ticklish matter how to give the former wife access to the money for the children's care while at the same time insuring that it will be used only for them.

One way to handle this would be a trust fund from which the trustee sends a monthly check for child support until the children reach the age of majority, usually age eighteen. The support check could go to the children after that. The entire trust could be turned over to them at the age the father feels they will be mature enough to handle a lump-sum payment, perhaps age twenty-one or even later.

Though the stepchildren, as a secondary responsibility, would not receive anything directly, they would be the indirect bene-factors of their mother's inheritance. It is up to her to decide what she will do with it. If she wants to do without and spend it on her children, that is her decision.

Adoption of the Stepchildren. When asked whether or not a stepfather should adopt stepchildren, many attorneys reply, "It depends on whom I'm representing. If I'm representing the natural mother, I encourage her to get the stepfather to adopt. Adoption laws enhance her child's security. However, if I'm representing the stepfather, I discourage it. The stepfather's primary attraction is the child's mother, not the child. Adoption suggests responsibility toward the child that the stepfather may not want to assume simply because the child is not his primary interest. He's just part of a package deal."

Though that might sound a bit cold and calculating, I have to agree with this in substance. If the stepfather would adopt the child whether or not he loved the child's mother, that would be another matter. But in most cases interest in the child is secondary.

The stepfather should also be careful that he is not sold on the notion that adopting the child will bring him closer to the child—that somehow it will remove the barriers that stepparenting throw in the way of a good relationship. If the stepfather cannot have a good relationship with the child as stepfather, it is doubtful that adoption would make any difference.

Sometimes adoption is brought up in discussions over what last name the child should use. One divorced mother got the California Supreme Court to consider her right to confer her maiden name on her children. She argued that it is confusing for the mother and children to have different names.

Some of the justices wondered what would happen if the mother remarried. Would the children's names be changed every time she changed husbands?

As it stands now, some states require the child to go by his or her legal birth name. Other states require the child to go by whatever name the custodial parent requests.

Personally I feel that the child should keep his legal birth name. First, it encourages the stepfamily to "come out of the closet" and identify itself as a stepfamily. Secondly, we have the continuing issue of loyalty. There is mystique in the biological bond. Yes, there is a lot of idealizing of the natural father, but it will not be corrected by changing the child's name. Let the child bear the name of the natural father. And let the stepfather win a place in the child's life not by court fiat but by the fact this child sees him as a decent human being and a worthy role model.

Incest and the Stepfamily. Roosevelt and Lofas tell the story about a stepfather, Bruce. His stepdaughter Kim was quite a flirt. She was also helpful and devoted to Bruce. It was getting more difficult not to respond to her—and tricky.

Nancy, her mother, didn't mind the competition. She realized that Kim was learning how to relate to men. But her stepfather was still young enough to have fantasies, and they bothered him. Kim would wear a minimal amount of clothing, and then she developed the habit of meeting him at the door with her lips puckered for a kiss. All she got was a fatherly peck on the cheek, but for Bruce the pressure was great.

"She isn't my daughter," Bruce thought. But then again, she was. She modeled herself after him and couldn't do enough to please him. But it was difficult not to get turned on. He wondered how many men actually get into trouble this way.[4]

Statistics on incest are unreliable. But it is estimated that 90 percent of all incest cases go unreported.[5] One researcher estimates that 19 percent of all   women and 8 percent of men were victimized as children.[6]

With the number of stepfamilies rapidly increasing through the decade of the eighties, I believe that we will find a growing problem with "stepfamily incest." Other researchers agree.[7] Technically, intercourse between a stepparent and stepchild is not incest, though it certainly is a crime. In the stepfamily, parents and children do not have the normal "incest taboo." Even though they constitute a stepfamily, they are not blood related.

Continuing sexual permissiveness in society also weakens the stepfamily's resistance to "stepfamily incest." Provocative dress and seductive behavior are seen everywhere. It's no wonder that the young woman in her teens wants to see if she has mastered the art and tries it out on her father—or stepfather. A certain amount of this is normal and to be expected. But society encourages an inappropriate expression of it in the family and weakens the incest taboo.

Both father and stepfather have an important responsibility at this point. On one hand it is proper to acknowledge that the girl is sexually potent, and it is also proper to let her know that *because* of her sexual potency she needs to be more discreet.

A father or stepfather often reacts destructively in an attempt to deal with his sexual feelings. He may ignore the girl or even become verbally abusive. He hopes to create distance from sexual temptation in this way.

A father or stepfather may be successful in creating distance, but he damages the girl's sense of self-worth and is likely to make her try even harder to seduce him—or any man—just to prove her sexual potency.

It is quite proper for the father or stepfather to say to the girl, "Honey, I wish you'd put more clothes on. You're growing up to be a very attractive woman, and your mother is all the woman I can handle right now." Mother can reinforce this by saying to her daughter, "Dad's coming home soon. I think he'd feel a little more at ease around you if you'd cover up a little more." With this approach both the mother and stepfather openly acknowledge the girl's sexual potency as a normal part of her growing up. The attitude is, "It's okay to be sexually potent. Just don't flaunt it."

In one giant step the girl has her femininity reinforced and gets a good lesson in sexual decorum.

A recent study of characteristics of father-daughter incestuous families should be of value to stepfamilies. In fact, if these characteristics exist in the natural family, I would say that the stepfamily should exercise even more vigilance since the natural-family incest taboo is absent.

According to this report in *Marriage and Divorce Today,* Judith Herman, M.D., and Lisa Hirschman, Ed.D., warn that there are certain circumstances that should alert us to the possibility of father-daughter incest.

> *"Whenever a mother is treated for severe chronic illness of any sort," they warn, "the family's adaptation to the mothers' disability should be assessed."*
>
> *The researchers examined case histories of 40 women (mean age 27.7) who had sexual relationships with their fathers during childhood. They also had a control group of 20 women (mean age 26.8) who recalled that their fathers had engaged in what the researchers term "seductive behavior," including peeping, exhibitionism and divulging sexual confidences. About three-quarters of the subjects' mothers were full-time housekeepers. The great majority of both groups' families were "intact" and "presented a conventional appearance," note the researchers. Over 90 percent of the cases had not been known to mental health or social service agency workers.*
>
> *Mothers in the incestuous families were more often described as seriously ill (55 percent vs. 15 percent) or disabled. Undiagnosed alcoholism, psychosis and depression were among the most commonly reported illnesses or disabilities. Thirty-eight percent of the incest group members had been separated from their mothers for fairly lengthy time periods during childhood; no control group member had been. The separations occurred because the mothers had been hospitalized or felt unable to rear children.[8]*

I have said nothing about stepmother-stepson incest. Though it is less frequent than father-daughter or stepfather-stepdaughter incest, I believe that in the decade of the eighties we will see it increase for the following reasons:

1. Absence of the natural-family incest taboo;
2. Earlier puberty of the boy, making him vulnerable longer as

a sexually potent male in the house with an adult female who is not his natural mother;

3. Less difference in age between the stepmother and son. Stepfathers tend to marry women younger than they. This means that a stepson generally is closer to the age of his stepmother than he would be in a natural family.

Families who are interested in becoming more aware of what they can do to avoid this problem may contact the Rape and Abuse Crisis Center, P.O. Box 1655, Fargo, ND 58107. They offer a preventative sex-education program called TOUCH for grade-school children, their parents, teachers, and school administrators. The initial program was developed for third- and fourth-grade children, because the mean age for sexual abuse is nine. They have an eleven-minute film entitled "Who Do You Tell?" The children are encouraged to share their reactions to the film. A coloring book called "Red Flag, Green Flag People" is also used to help the children to talk about touching—particularly any that's confusing or frightening. They are encouraged to talk about anyone they are having "touching problems" with.

Pastors would perform a valuable service to members of their congregations by checking into this program. From what I know about the materials mentioned above, I believe that they could be plugged into the church educational program in a discreet way.

Stepfamilies will also want to look at item 36 on the Stepparent Test. Don't avoid answering this item honestly. And by all means, talk about it if you feel uneasy about stepparent-stepchild sexual behavior.

9.

What to Expect of a Stepchild

A parent and stepparent should have expectations of the stepchild in their new family. Everyone must cooperate in making a new family system work.

But I don't want this chapter title to mislead you. Whether or not the stepchild fulfills these expectations depends largely on the adult leadership in the home. As a family therapist I commonly run into a problem with both the natural family and stepfamily where the child, who is disrupting the household, is brought in by the parents who tell me in so many words, "Here is your patient. Fix him!"

It's not quite that simple. Anyone who knows anything about family systems knows that the child may be the "indicated patient," but it is the whole family that needs therapy. What the parent and stepparent are or are not doing at home has a tremendous influence on what the child does or does not do. I am not saying that the parents should always be blamed if they have troubled children. The child has a responsibility for his decisions too. What I am saying is that the parents are responsible for creating an atmosphere in the home that will lend itself to successful family interaction. Having done that, the destructive choices the child makes will cause a minimum of damage to himself and to the system. Parental leadership also offers the best prospect for the maturity of the child.

Sometimes parents must exercise "tough love"—a balance of firmness and no-nonsense caring about the child. It is a concept that is regaining popularity among family therapists.

People magazine carried a story on the work of David and Phyllis York, who have formed an organization of parents called "Toughlove." The Yorks came to this place out of desperation.

> *"For a long time I denied that my kids really didn't give a damn about me and the family," says David York. "They were selfish. . . . The essence of our philosophy is that parents must take a stand with their children. . . . Teenagers must learn to accept the consequences of their actions, and parents must stop trying to protect them."*[1]

I am not suggesting that all children need this kind of firmness. I have already warned of creating the "too-good child." Yet parents and stepparents who establish themselves as the leaders in the home and who are accepted as leaders are in the best position to have their expectations of the stepchild met. They must have the toughness of character to go as far as the Yorks did if they must. The Yorks believe that sometimes this means that the runaway child is not let back into the house until he gets his act together. Sometimes it means taking the child to court. This is a side of love not often practiced in families.

Dos and Don'ts for Parents and Stepparents

Parents and stepparents who accept the responsibility for leadership in the home should first be aware of some dos and don'ts. Below is a digest of suggestions made in the booklet "Yours, Mine and Ours: Tips for Stepparents."

Dos and Don'ts About Marriage. Whether you are contemplating marrying someone with children or you have already done so, consider the following:

• *Do* examine your motives and those of your spouse (present or future) for marrying. Understanding your motives will help you deal with unrealistic expectations and disappointments, many of which involve the children and stepchildren and how you raise them.

• *Do* get to know your spouse (present or future). Face squarely your contrasting lifestyles, and talk about the modifications you need to make in bringing two families together.

• *Don't* place your children in the position of making a decision about your remarriage or approving of the marriage if it is a *fait accompli*.

• *Do* try to anticipate the financial problems remarriage creates. Openly discuss your concerns. Silence will only lead to a building of resentment and an eventual explosion that most certainly will be destructive.

Dos and Don'ts About the Children.

• *Do* give the children the time they need—to mourn the loss of the absent parent, to adjust, to accept, and to belong to a new family system.

• *Do* expect the children to have some problems adjusting from a single parent to a stepfamily situation. Understand their problems, but don't try to overcompensate.

• *Don't* try to replace a lost parent. Be an additional parent figure.

• *Do* accept the children's loyalty to the absent parent. Children of divorce can have good relationships with both stepparents and natural parents.

Dos and Don'ts About Parenting.

• *Don't* expect too much too soon, either from yourself or from the stepchildren. Stepparenting isn't easy.

• *Do* help your child and your new spouse to understand that your relationships with both are valuable but different. One cannot replace the other.

• *Do* recognize that you may be compared with the absent parent. Be prepared to be tested, manipulated, and challenged in your new role.

• *Don't* retreat from a child's challenge. Children need the security of a firm and fair response.

• *Do* back up your spouse on childrearing issues. Rearing children is tough. Rearing someone else's children is tougher.

• *Do* decide, with your mate, what is best for your children and stand by it. It frightens children when they can successfully manipulate adults.

• *Do* acknowledge periods of cooperation among stepsiblings. Try to treat stepchildren and your own with equal fairness.

• *Do* communicate! Don't pretend that everything is fine when it isn't. Acknowledge problems immediately and deal with them openly.

You may find it helpful to make several copies of this list of dos and don'ts and periodically evaluate how well you're doing as a stepfamily. Both the husband and wife should do the checklist. Try to get the children involved too, especially if they are junior-high age or older.

The purpose of the exercise is not to condemn or to find fault. It is to exchange information about how each member of the family feels about these important issues and why. It should be done in a nonattacking and nondefensive way.

If the family mood is tense, you may establish the ground rule that each person will simply make a statement and that no interaction will be permitted. If the mood is not tense, you may want to discuss the issues. But, again, be careful that the mood is nonattacking and nondefensive. If attacking, defensive behavior creeps in, return to the rule of making statements with no interaction.

If the tension is so great that the husband and wife cannot even make statements, each should complete the list privately and then exchange copies and read them privately. If one spouse will not cooperate, the other spouse should try anyway. Write a note and attach the checklist.

Understand the Stepchild

If the stepparent expects success with the stepchild, then he or she must understand what goes on inside the child. Every stepparent (and parent) must understand what I call "the stepchild's emotional cluster"—a variety of feelings, each of which interrelates or clusters, building on each other to make the child behave as he does. I have identified five. They are (1) death, divorce, and guilt; (2) a question of loyalty; (3) the biological bond; (4) idealization; and (5) conflict over name. Let's look at these individually.

Death, Divorce, and Guilt. Starting chronologically, death, divorce, and guilt constitute the first element in the cluster. The child has experienced the loss of a parent and often feels guilty about it. This is true even if the parent has died. Sometimes the child entertains the notion that he might have been the cause of the parent's untimely death. How many times parents say thoughtless things like, "If you keep that up, you'll send me to an early grave"!

The child may feel guilty because he had not shown the deceased parent proper appreciation when the parent was alive. He thinks that perhaps he can make up for it by keeping the memory of that parent alive. Remarriage is a terrible reality for the child who is not willing to face the fact that the other parent is dead. This is the first shock the child faces. The parent *really is dead*. A stepparent is now living here. Out of this often comes anger not only at the stepparent, who is an "intruder," but also anger at the living parent for not being "faithful" to the dead parent. I have known *adult* children to have problems with this as well.

In the case of the divorced parent, the child may feel that he was responsible for the divorce, but that maybe he can get mom and dad back together again. Maybe he can make up for the damage he has done. This feeling accounts for a great deal of otherwise unexplainable behavior in children. It's incredible the lengths to which they go to accuse themselves and also to assuage their guilt.

A Question of Loyalty. The guilt of the child naturally gives rise to the question of loyalty, particularly in the case of divorce (rather than death) and remarriage. The child often feels that acceptance of and obedience to the stepparent would be interpreted as disloyalty to the natural, noncustodial parent. And I have known noncustodial parents to play on the issue of loyalty because of their own neurotic reaction to the divorce. This is why stepchildren often do not show love and appreciation to the stepparent. They imagine that it would show disloyalty to the absent parent (see Stepparent Test nos. 6 and 7).

Children secretly hope their parents will get back together. But a parent's remarriage is a terrible reality. The dream of reconciliation is shattered. The child's attitude toward the stepparent seems to be, "My father (or mother) may have accepted you, but I want you to know I'll never accept you. My real mom and dad belong together!"

The stepparent may have to accept this as a reality. But he or she must recognize that the child's rejection, anger, and disobedience have nothing to do with the stepparent personally. The behavior is the result of an unresolved conflict over the breakup of the marriage. No matter who became the stepparent, the child would still hate him.

This is where the stepparent, in disciplining the child, must understand the real issue. He must take the position with the child that says, "I understand where you're coming from. You feel as though I'm an intruder, and you want to be loyal to your real parent. That's okay. But we need to have an understanding. I have a responsibility to be the male (or female) head of the house. And because of this I need your cooperation and obedience. I know I'll never replace your dad (or mom), and I don't plan to try. But so long as we live together, it will be a lot easier on all of us to accept the fact that I'm here to stay. Nothing you do is going to drive me away." I'll have more to say about this later under "discipline."

Biological Bond. The loyalty of the child rises not only from feelings of guilt but also from a lot of romantic nonsense about the biological bond. The stock phrase is "Parents love their children." Is that so? Then how do you explain the mother who throws her baby into a trash can? Or consider the prevalence of child abuse. Many of the kids called "runaways" who roam the country are really "throwaways." The reason they don't go home is that *they know they're not wanted*! I'm not talking about "tough love" situations where the kids are told that they will have to straighten up if they come home. The parents of many runaways want them under no circumstances.

The truth is that parents do not always love their children, yet the myth goes on. Is it any wonder that a child will hang on to the idea even though the absent parent never visits and continually breaks promises? The child fantasizes a bond of love that simply does not exist. This is why it is important not to tear down the absent parent (see Stepparent Test nos. 29 and 30). If you do, you will create animosity in the child and force him deeper into his unrealistic view of the absent parent. Of course neither do you want to go to the other extreme and create an unrealistic image of the absent parent. That's confusing. The child will wonder, if the absent parent is so great, why did you get a divorce? What is more, the child will doubt his own view of reality when he sees the absent parent more realistically. It is better to take a noncommittal stance. The child will see the truth when he is old enough.

Idealization. It is only natural that from this should come an idealized view of the absent parent. Not only does the child have an unrealistic view of the parent's love, he also imagines the absent parent as a great person who can do everything better than anyone else.

This is why dad always catches more fish than stepdad. Mom's lasagna is always better than stepmom's (see Stepparent Test nos. 6 and 7). If you don't get the love and appreciation you want as a stepparent, perhaps it will help to realize that the child probably is idealizing the parent. It is difficult enough for a child to face the loss of a parent without having to face the reality that the stepparent may really be doing a superior job.

You are the adult. When you feel angry over the child's ingratitude, just remember, the child can take only so much reality. Give him time. True love bears the burden with him (1 Cor. 13).

Conflict Over Name. The final element in this "emotional cluster" is conflict over name—the child's own name and what to call the stepparent. I have already discussed the issue of the child's name in connection with adoption in the previous chapter. I believe it is best for the child to retain his/her legal birth name. If stepfamilies are going to come out of the closet and be identified as such, let's get started with names. When the parents are matter-of-fact about the child's having a different last name than theirs, it gives the child the message that it's okay to have a different name and to be part of a stepfamily.

But what does the child call the stepparent? Most stepchildren resent calling the parent "mom" or "dad," though sometimes an affection grows to the place where this happens. This should be at the child's initiative.

Some children settle on first names, though many experts feel that such familiarity erodes the authority of the stepparent. I would judge this on individual merit. A strong, well-adjusted stepparent could handle it.

Others use titles in conjunction with the first name, as in "Papa Fred" or "Mama Jean." Sometimes the name is left off and just a title is used like "Ma" or "Pa." Multi-generation families do this. In my family we have to help the children sort out father, grandfather, and great-grandfather. We use the names "Pop" (great-grandfather), "Granddaddy" (grandfather), and "Daddy" (father).

The best policy is not to force the issue of names. The child will develop a manner of address over a period of time that he feels comfortable with. Just be careful, as the stepparent, that you don't take offense at the child's bewilderment over what to call you. Remember, he is wrestling with guilt, loyalty, biological bond, and idealization. The problem with name is part of this "emotional cluster."

The Stepparent As Authority

Throughout this book I have asserted that stepfamilies are different from natural families. But I also caution that we run a great risk when we make them so different that we fail to apply the usual rules that govern well-ordered families. Nowhere is this issue so important as with the issue we face now—the stepparent as authority.

The words *authority* and *control* were unpopular for many years in family therapy. But they are making a comeback. What place does the stepparent have in the scheme of things concerning authority and control? Is there any similarity in the rules that govern natural parenting and stepparenting? I think there are.

The Importance of a United Front. A cardinal rule in natural parenting is the rule of the united front. I believe that this must be applied in stepparenting. Parents and stepparents must be in agreement on what they expect of the children before they can hope to have the cooperation and obedience of the children.

The first sin in the universe was the sin of self-will. This was Lucifer's sin against God (Isa. 14:12–15). It was the first sin in the Garden of Eden. God told Adam and Eve not to eat of the fruit of the Tree of Knowledge of Good and Evil, but they exercised *self-will* and disobeyed.

The sin of self-will is the foundational problem between parents and children. It is the exercise of self against the parent. The parent is part of the problem when the child is not handled wisely. When the problem is effectively dealt with in family life, the child is prepared to enter a society that does not tolerate self-will.

Parents and stepparents must therefore present a united front to the children. This involves at least two things:

1. The parent and stepparent should talk privately about their expectations so their differences may be aired without the child's knowing anything about them. The child cannot challenge, manipulate, or exploit differences he or she is ignorant of.

2. Though the parent and stepparent may disagree over an on-the-spot decision one of them makes, the other should support it until they can iron out the differences *privately*. Disagreements over how to raise the child are *their* business, not the child's.

Children will generally test a stepparent and challenge his or her authority. The child may say, "You're not my real father. You can't tell me what to do." One stepfather said that the first time his stepson said that to him, he was stunned. But the boy's mother backed up her husband, and it didn't happen again.

Stepparents aren't the only ones who have trouble presenting a united front. Over the years I have counseled scores of natural parents who wrestle with this problem. The degree to which they were successful in achieving agreement as parents was the degree to which they succeeded in controlling their children. I have no statistics, but I have a theory that stepparents probably don't disagree on how to handle their children much more frequently than natural parents. I say this to discourage stepparents from making the excuse, "Of course we can't agree on how to handle the kids; we're a *step*family."

I'm sure a parent will say, "But you don't expect me to stand by while my child suffers physical abuse, do you?" No, I don't, any more than I would suggest this be done in the natural family. Any situation that gets out of hand should be defused by the uninvolved adult, natural or step. All I'm saying is, don't be too quick to erode the image of the united front. If it is a borderline situation, you may go to your child privately and comfort him. Suppose, for example, the child has been ignored by his stepfather. It would be entirely appropriate for the mother to say to the child, "I know you wanted Papa Fred to be proud of your good report card. He's just so tired tonight, he can't give any more." This kind of thing is done in natural families all the time—one of the parents' putting oil on the water.

In the case just mentioned, it would be wise for mother not to give Papa Fred the cold shoulder for mistreating her child but rather say to him, "Honey, you look beat. If you want, I'll try to keep the kids out of your way." Your child and your husband both need to know that you understand them.

Kicking the Blaming Habit. Another thing that can facilitate a united front is to kick the blaming habit. A parent will often keep the stepparent from doing his or her job because of guilt. The parent feels guilty over what the divorce has done to the child or what the child has suffered because he or she has been deprived of love. The parent feels that the poor child should not be expected to behave as other children because he has been the victim of cruel circumstances.

Children are far more resilient than parents give them credit for. In fact, many children wouldn't know that they are to be pitied, protected, and indulged unless the guilt-ridden parents told them.

Blaming not only keeps the parent from administering effective discipline, but it also gives the child an excuse not to behave. Adults don't mean to give this message, but this is what children are hearing them say: We all *know* why children get drunk, stoned, shoplift, steal cars, get pregnant, and commit a score of other crimes. They have come from broken homes!

Nonsense! What about the child from a broken home who becomes a U.S. senator? The answer is that he probably didn't know he was to be pitied and got on with the business of life. He just didn't know that he had an excuse to fail! Don't give your child or stepchild an excuse to fail.

Who's in Charge Here? Effective stepparenting begins with a firm attitude on the part of the natural parent and the stepparent. It is an attitude that says to the children, "Hey, gang, we want you to know that we hope this will be a big, happy family. But a family isn't a democracy—one person, one vote. We will be sensitive to your wants and needs, but ultimately, we have to take responsibility for what happens here. And therefore we need to make it clear that we're in charge."

The May 1980 issue of *Families,* a Reader's Digest publication, ran an article called "The Secret of Stepping." The refreshing thing about the article is that the author, John Leonard, says that he is tired of all the articles expounding the difficulties, resentments, and problems of stepfamilies. He wants to establish that stepparents, from the start, are to bring maturity and leadership to the family. Says Leonard:

> *Being a stepparent is not being mellow. Among other things, a stepfamily is a series of trade-offs. . . .*
>
> *You make rules, but you explain why. . . . If you are angry or just plain tired, you tell why. If you are pleased, you say so instead of grunting. . . . You remember to apologize.*
>
> *You do a lot of listening, whether or not you are interested. . . . You will be firm, but you will not be sarcastic. . . .*
>
> *What are you doing? You are treating the child like another human being, not a vassal. The result is amazing. We owe our children something: their dignity. Then maybe they will love us.* [2]

Being "in charge" means establishing boundaries and yet giving freedom to the child to express himself fully within those boundaries. This is the way God deals with us as adults. He puts moral boundaries around us. To step outside is, in family terms, a challenge to the Father's authority. We are chastised for that challenge. But we are free to live as we wish so long as we stay within those boundaries. It is true that we may not always choose to exercise that freedom for the good of others in the family (Rom. 14:1–15:7; 1 Cor. 8–11). But we do have freedom within boundaries.

Tough Love. I have mentioned already the concept of "tough love." Tough love follows the biblical principle of chastisement as an act of love. You love someone enough to let him suffer the painful consequences of his behavior.

American parents have an anemic love. In the name of "love"

they will not permit their children to suffer the consequences of their misbehavior.

The Yorks, whom I mentioned earlier as the founders of the organization "Toughlove," tell the story of one of their daughters and how they handled her with tough love. *People* magazine reports:

> *"We were a close family. Then all of a sudden the bottom dropped out. I thought, what happened to those sweet little girls? I kept trying to be reasonable, even when it wasn't working. . . . One of the girls was always stoned, sleeping all morning, not doing well in school. We knew all three were unhappy."*
>
> *Just before Christmas 1976, one of the girls was arrested for holding up a cocaine dealer. It was her second such offense, and when she called home expecting to be bailed out, her parents refused. "We couldn't take it anymore," David explains. "We said, 'You got yourself into this; you get yourself out.' We hung up and then just sat there and cried." The daughter was locked up for six weeks. The Yorks did not visit, but sent some close friends to check on her. After she was released (she was acquitted), her parents refused to see her until she straightened herself out. She spent four months in a halfway house.*
>
> *A noticeably subdued, cooperative daughter and Toughlove were the results of these hard-nosed tactics.*[3]

Perhaps this love is tougher than you care to employ—or even need to employ. But catch the spirit of what they are doing. The Yorks needed to get the message across that they were in charge.

Get These and You've Got It All. Though authority, control, and tough love are important aspects of parenting and step-parenting, I don't want you, the stepparent, to get the idea that you are going to be able to secure compliance with everything you want from the child. You must be careful not to make the mistake many natural parents make. In their attempt to control the child, many parents hassle them about everything—eating junk food; the music they listen to; their manners; the way they dress, wear their hair, and keep their room. I'm not saying that these things are unimportant. But you must be careful not to try to get everything all at once.

Every human being has what I call "a hassle limit." We can

stand to be hassled about only so many things for so long until we rebel. There is no sense encouraging rebellion when we don't have to.

I believe that there are three things that a parent and stepparent *must* have from the child. If you have these, you will get everything else in a matter of time.

- Respect and obedience
- Accountability
- Control over friends

Let's look at these individually.

1. Respect and obedience. The stepparent has a legitimate place of authority in the life of the stepchild, just as teachers, police officers, camp counselors, and schoolbus drivers. The task of the parent and stepparent is to help the child understand and accept this. The stepparent who attempts to be fair and reasonable and has the backing of the parent is in the best position to gain the child's respect and obedience (see Stepparent Test nos. 12, 13, 17–22, 25). Note that I do not say "love" and "appreciation." These may never come because of loyalty conflict (test nos. 6 and 7).

A calm firmness is also essential. It is an attitude that says, "I accept the responsibility to be in charge, and I can handle that responsibility" (test nos. 4, 9, 10).

The stepparent who would gain the authority and respect of the stepchild cannot worry about being liked by the child. His major concern must be effective parenting. Sometimes out of fear of not being liked, the parent and stepparent get bogged down in discussions with the child over what's fair or not fair. If the parent and stepparent have agreed on a course of action and have considered the child's feelings, the child must understand that's the way it is. The child doesn't have to like it or even think that it is fair. Insubordination to either the parent or the stepparent must be regarded as a serious breach of organizational discipline. The child may present his case in reasonable tones. But once he has presented his case and the parental decision is made, chipping away at the parent or stepparent with further arguments or throwing temper tantrums must be viewed as insubordination.

Too often parents and stepparents in attempting to be fair give the child an unrealistic view of life and keep the child from developing an ability to cope with unfairness in a socially acceptable way. Children need to learn that *life isn't always fair*. And if they expect society to go out of its way to be sure it is being fair to the child, he or she had better be prepared to face a harsh reality. The parent and stepparent should give fairness a reasonable try but not lose sleep over accusations that they are not being fair.

I may sound harsh, but it's axiomatic that the degree to which authority has the subordination of its people is the degree to which that authority is an effective control.

2. Accountability. Accountability is simply the responsibility that each member of the family has to the others to disclose where he is going and what he will be doing. The parent and stepparent owe it to each other and to the child, as does the child to the parent and stepparent.

Accountability is built on the principle that trust is essential in family relations. If we are going to live with each other and count on each other for our well-being, then we have to trust each other. But we can't trust each other if we're always worrying about ugly surprises. If we're going to avoid such surprises, then we should freely disclose where we are going and what we will be doing.

It is fairly easy to maintain accountability with small children. It's when children are older and are free to be away from home for long periods of time that it becomes an issue.

If the child feels it necessary to lie about his whereabouts or what he is doing, it probably indicates that he thinks the parent or stepparent will disapprove. But perhaps the child thinks you will disapprove because you seem to disapprove of *everything* he does. Here is where we need to consider the hassle factor I spoke of earlier. The child must know that you feel you are reasonable and that you have a perfect right to determine whether or not you approve of where he is going and what he's going to do.

Truth in accountability is so important to family trust that the children must understand that it is a big item. The parent and stepparent must have it with each other, and they must have it with each child.

What happens if your child lies to you? He must understand

that the issue is not simply that he went over to his buddy's house instead of going to the library. The issue is a violation of trust and the insecurity that rises from it. It is not a happy family situation when the parent and stepparent never know when the child leaves the house what he really is going to do or where he really is going and if they will be confronted with any ugly surprises.

One final word on accountability. Don't fall for the "you don't trust me" gambit. My answer to that is, "You are not different from me. Any human being who wants to misbehave will misbehave if he thinks he can get away with it. Accountability makes it easier for you to behave and makes it easier for me to trust. When you are willingly and gladly accountable, I have less need for accountability because your attitude strengthens my trust. Trust is not a psychological exercise. It is directly related to trustworthy behavior."

3. Friends. As your child grows up and grows away from home, peer influence more than anything else will affect his attitude and moral development. You should make sure he knows how to choose friends.

Stepparents are especially blessed when they are able to start with young stepchildren and guide the children's choice of friends early in life. But this is not always the case. Stepparents often face working with children who already have a well-established way of choosing friends—friends who are not always wholesome.

Whenever I talk to families, both natural and step, about the importance of this, the child or teen tells me, "My parents aren't going to choose my friends." I respond, "I agree with you. They should *not* choose your friends. But they have the right and responsibility to *veto* any friends they feel are a bad influence. And if it turns out that you keep choosing friends who are vetoed, you may lead a lonely life."

You may wonder how to enforce something like this. My answer is, "Tough love, parent; tough love." Can you be the kind of parent or stepparent who is fair and firm, who sticks by his guns in a calm, cool manner? Are you willing, if you can't solve this problem as a family, to seek family counsel and make sure your child goes too? You have the clout if you'll use it.

It is my experience that when a parent and stepparent are able to receive from the child respect and obedience, accountability, and control of friends, the other concerns such as dress, studies, a tidy bedroom, and taste in music are much easier to deal with. These become less urgent issues and are seen as refinements of a child who already wants to pattern his or her life after the parent and stepparent. Do not make the mistake of hassling the child about everything. Start with what is most important.

Other Children in the Household. The stepchild may find that he or she has to share the home with stepbrothers and stepsisters. This raises three important issues:

- The fiction of equal love
- Sibling rivalry
- Sex and stepchildren

Let us examine these problems:

1. The fiction of equal love. Equal love *is* a fiction. For the stepparent to suppose that the children and stepchildren will all experience the same kind of love from the parent and stepparent is nonsense.

Let's face it. All children do not behave in a manner that encourages affection or the display of it. For example, Suzie says to her stepmother, "You don't love me. You're nicer to Lisa [her stepsister] than you are to me." Stepmother should reply, "You're right, Suzie. I feel a lot more comfortable with Lisa than I do with you. She's usually pleasant and cooperative and not angry and demanding. Suzie, when I hear you get angry and demanding, I don't want to be around you."

Note that it is the *behavior,* not the *person,* who is unacceptable. This response is far different from, "You're right, Suzie. You're an obnoxious brat. Your father may spoil you, but I will not!"

Stepchildren often try the same tactics that minorities sometimes use. "You don't like me because I'm (black, Jewish, Mexican, Oriental, Irish, or Slavic)." "Racism" is an epithet frequently thrown out to obscure the fact that the person is rejected simply because he or she behaves badly and is unpleasant to be near.

The most loving thing the stepmother can do for Suzie is not to respond to her with the same kind of love she gives Lisa. Stepmother does love Suzie, *but it's a different kind of love*. It's tough love. It's the kind of love that says, "I don't like the behavior. I find it difficult to live with it. But I care enough about you, Suzie, to tell you what my problem is and, I hope, to help you develop a new approach to people that won't make you feel rejected." Love takes different forms. Sometimes it is a display of affection. Other times it is firm patience and a willingness to do a very difficult job—to stepparent a stepchild whose behavior is abominable (see test nos. 1–4, 9, 10, 16–25, 28, 37, 38, 42, 43).

2. Sibling rivalry. Rivalry between children in the natural family is common, and the basic ingredient is self-interest. Each child jockeys to get the biggest, best, and most for himself.

The same thing happens in stepfamilies. But often accusations of favoritism are hurled. Poor Johnny comes up on the short end because he's the *step*child, and so it goes.

Now it's true that favoritism often does occur, and the parent and stepparent must honestly face this possibility (see test nos. 11, 12, 15). But too often it is the child's behavior, not his step-position, that is to blame.

Take the case of Brenda, age twelve. She was left in charge of cutting her stepbrother's birthday cake and serving it to him, her two sisters, and herself. She gave the three of them half the cake and took the other half for herself.

Carol, her stepmother, said, "I believe that her dad has encouraged this. He always tried to be too fair with them—to see that no one came up short. But instead of encouraging fairness, he actually raised the concern that someone might come up short. He taught the kids to jealously guard their own interests and get what they can when they can."

Carol was right. And she was also right when she said, "My way of doing it is that if anyone complains, that person does without. And when it comes to arguments, I'm not going to be referee. If they can't get along, they'll be separated. They'll soon learn that they'd better solve their own problems with each other if they're going to be allowed to be together. I find that they really are social creatures and would rather be together. And they will solve their problems if we let them."

3. Sex and stepchildren. Because stepbrothers and stepsisters are not related by blood, there is a greater likelihood of sex play in the stepfamily than in the natural family. But the guilt can be just as damaging.

Stepparents and parents would do well to help the children cope with this temptation. I'm not talking about wild-eyed suspicion over the most innocent act or remark but a calm setting and enforcing of boundaries. The book *Living in Step* offers an excellent discussion of "sex and step."[4] I have mentioned some of the suggestions below.

When the parents leave the children at home, an older woman might be invited to "house sit." Sexual decorum is important—no running around in underwear or a bathtowel. Also, after a certain hour everybody must be settled down in his or her own room. Having the same-sex children share a room helps monitor the situation.

The attitude of the natural parent and stepparent is crucial. *Because* we have normal sexual instincts, we must have rules of conduct. It is not a matter of, "You'd better not. . . ." It's a matter of, "We expect you to have normal sexual reflexes; and *because of them,* we don't want to create unnecessary stimulation by the way we live together."

Helps for Stepchildren. Stepparents should be aware of a helpful monthly newsletter called *Stepparent News.* It offers a digest of timely articles and also carries a feature for children called "Stepping Stones." Stepparents may find it helpful to read the feature, have the stepchild read it, and then discuss it together. It is not a Christian publication, but it offers many valuable insights into the needs of stepfamilies.

10.

The Rest of the Cast of Characters and How to Handle Them

Remember Eddie in chapter 1? Both of his parents divorced and remarried, and the resulting natural and step relationships presented him with quite an imposing cast of characters who had an impact on his life. The men in the cast were his father, stepfather, and his stepmother's former husband. The women were his mother, his maternal grandmother, his stepmother, and his stepmother's ex-husband's wife!

It is true that the *natural extended family* made up of grandparents, aunts, and uncles often have an influence on the child. But we really can't compare this to what happens in the stepfamily, where *by court order* your child periodically visits or lives with people in the cast whom you may not like and who may have a negative impact on your child's life.

In this chapter I not only want to help the stepfamily know how to handle this large cast of characters, but I also want to appeal to those who are outside the immediate stepfamily to consider the welfare of the child or children in all that they do and say. Yes, there has been a divorce. And it probably wasn't a "nice divorce"—few of them are. It is likely that the extended families have taken sides; and even though the divorce is final and one or both of the spouses has remarried, the battle goes on through the children. If, as you say, you have the best interests of the children at heart, please give careful attention to this chapter.

You are in a position to do great good or great harm.

When I refer to "the rest of the cast of characters," I have in mind everyone in the extended family and stepfamily system other than the custodial parent, stepparent, and custodial children. But I do want to say to the stepparent and parent who have custody that you have a responsibility to relate to the rest of the cast in a considerate manner that also takes into account the feelings of the children. *You* may detest your former spouse, but your child still loves that parent.

When I talk about "handling" the rest of the cast of characters, I mean relating to them with the child's feelings and best interest in mind. You have divorced your former spouse, but your child hasn't. The child's love, loyalty, and idealization may go beyond reason. And even though you don't think your former spouse deserves the child's devotion, that is how the child feels. My appeal is to both the custodial family and the noncustodial family: If you love the child as you say you do, then behave in a manner that takes his feelings and best interests into consideration.

The Noncustodial Parent and Stepparent

The most frequent contact the custodial child has with the extended stepfamily is with the noncustodial parent and noncustodial stepparent. Most divorce settlements provide the noncustodial parent with "reasonable visitation rights." The ambiguity of this provision is both helpful and unhelpful. It leaves the parents to decide what is "reasonable." But since they have probably both been unreasonable with each other throughout the divorce proceedings, this may be a further source of conflict. What is helpful about it is that it gives the parents complete freedom to work out a visitation plan that fits their particular situation.

The Custodial Child and the Noncustodial Parent. The most common agreement between parents who live near each other is for the child to visit the noncustodial parent every other weekend, usually Friday after school to Sunday evening. Holidays such as Thanksgiving, Christmas, and Easter are rotated. The child will spend Christmas one year with one parent and the next year with the other parent.

1. The child's needs. Though the parents may be making an attempt to be fair to each other, they also need to give careful thought to how the child feels about the visitation arrangements. It is far better for the parents to bear inequity for the sake of the child than to insist on "parental rights" to the neglect of the child's rights. The courts tend to agree.

The parents may not be in the best position to find out what the child wants in the matter of visitation. The child, attempting to avoid loyalty conflict with the parents, will probably tell them that he doesn't know what he wants. Or he may tell each parent what he thinks that parent wants to hear. A neutral party—such as a pastor, physician, or family therapist—should attempt to find out what the child wants in the matter of visitation. It should be remembered that the child is going to do his best to assume neutrality in the matter even though he may have some very negative feelings about one of the parents. Generally, it is helpful for the child to have regular contact with both parents. It is his way of assuring himself that even though mom and dad have divorced, they still are mom and dad. I say "generally" because, in evaluating your stepfamily system, you may find that this is not in your child's best interest. The child may not really want to live with the custodial parent, or he may not want to visit the noncustodial parent. Again, what does the *child* want?

2. The noncustodial mother's needs. It is important not only to understand the child's needs but also the noncustodial mother's needs. She may be a single noncustodial parent or she may have remarried. But understanding how she is feeling will eventually help the child who visits her. Her former husband, the custodial father, and his new wife may not like her. In fact, they may resent having to let the child see her; but they need to know where she is in her world of reality so they can understand her impact on the child. You can help your children adjust to visitation problems when you understand what *is* rather than doggedly insist on what *ought* to be.

Consider, for example, Sally, a single noncustodial parent, who found it difficult to cope with her former husband's remarriage and her children's new stepmother. At a recent singles conference she shared a poem about it, entitled "Feeling Threatened":

Who are you
That sleep with my husband?
Why do you seek my place, my name?
Do you also want my kids?

What gives you the right?
I bore them.
My body nurtured and delivered them—
Offerings to my husband.

One by one, you steal my loved ones.
God gave me *my husband;*
He gave me *four children.*
Are you smarter than God that
* you try to take these from me?*
                                        —Sally Leep[1]

Whether or not you think Sally should feel this way, she does. Moreover, her feelings are going to affect the way she relates to the children when they visit. If she feels that their stepmother is trying to supplant her, she may become overly possessive and jealous of the children's loyalty. Anything good the children say about their stepmother may make her feel all the more threatened. She is in danger of reacting badly and speaking against both stepmother and father when the children visit her.

Though she may be indulging her need to feel more secure with her children, she most certainly will damage her relationship with them and disrupt their relationship with their father and step-mother. I can't tell the noncustodial mother *not* to feel that way. She can't simply turn off her feelings. But she can keep herself from acting out destructive behavior and saying destructive things. If she really has the best interests of her children at heart, she will keep their welfare in mind. If she finds that her bitterness and jealousy spill out every time the children visit her, she should receive therapy to work out the bitterness.

If she has remarried, she will create problems for her new husband if she behaves badly. He certainly won't want to see her children come to visit if it makes her a wreck every time they come. She most assuredly will have a negative influence on his behavior toward the children. They will pick up in his attitude, "I wish you weren't here."

One of the most difficult things the noncustodial mother must contend with is the general reaction of society and the specific reaction of her family when she *chooses* not to have custody—an empty nest by choice, as it is often called.

Society's traditional view of motherhood is that she is the primary caretaker and, in the event of divorce, the custodial parent. The courts have supported this notion since 1900 with their "doctrine of tender years," which says a young child belongs with his mother unless she is declared unfit. The attitude of the courts has changed in recent years. Now "the interest of the child" is of primary concern.

Not only are the courts having second thoughts about a mother's being the more suitable parent for young children, mothers themselves are wondering about that too. According to Tobey Milne, psychotherapist in Vienna, Virginia, a mother may choose the empty nest for a variety of reasons:

1. She often feels almost totally responsible for the breakdown of the marriage and therefore has no right to ask for child custody.

2. She wants to avoid a custody battle.

3. She feels a lack of emotional support in her role as mother. She feels she can't do it alone.

4. She has extreme feelings of non-worth as wife, mother, and person.

5. She is afraid that her low self-worth may rub off on her children or hurt them in some way.

6. She feels economic pressure. Only 49 percent of mothers actually receive the child support the courts mandate.

7. Anger at the husband for not assuming his responsibility as a parent over the years. Now he can do it all!

8. She would rather build her own career and find self-worth in that than in being a single custodial parent.[2]

Though 90 percent of custody suits are settled out of court, the noncustodial mother still feels a social stigma—"You abandoned your children!" What makes it worse is that her own mother is often her sharpest critic, saying such things as, "I didn't have a happy marriage, but I stayed with *my* kids. And even after your father left I made a life for *you*! Where would you be today if I had given up custody of you?'' And if her mother doesn't say that in so many words, the implication is obvious.

Noncustodial mothers have a great emotional adjustment to make. Not only do they have to mourn the loss of the marriage and loss of the children, they must face the children's confusion and hurt over her leaving them and the "bad mother" label her former husband hangs on her.

In rebuilding her life, she must see herself as a worthwhile person apart from her role as her parents' daughter or her children's mother. She is worthwhile as an individual *unattached to a family,* not an easy position in a couple-oriented society. It may take several years to get to that place, but this must be her goal, particularly if she chooses to remain unmarried.

I strongly urge noncustodial mothers and noncustodial fathers to seek the support of single groups. It is true that many of the groups include never-marrieds and widows or widowers. But there are many single parents and single noncustodial parents in these groups.[3]

Three years after she left her children, a mother wrote to them the following letter. She acknowledged that the separation was painful, and said,

> *This is difficult for all of us. . . . You are part of my life and will be always. . . . In future years, when you are grown, there would have come a time when you would have to leave me and go on to live a life on your own, but our separation was so premature. I let go of you before either of us was ready. . . . I care about you every day. I care that your body is well. I care that your emotions and mind are well, just like when I lived with you. I love you as much as always. I am here whenever you need me. I am either one ring away on the phone or one hour away in my car, but I am as close to you as your skin. In my heart, I love you . . . MOM.[4]*

3. The noncustodial father's needs. Rick was a good provider and hard worker. He believed that his wife was doing a good job of raising the children and that everyone in the family was fairly content.

He wasn't prepared for the shock he received when he returned from a business trip. His wife and kids were gone, and the note left behind simply said, "We've gone to mother's. We'll be staying here until my lawyer can make arrangements for separate maintainence. I care about you as a person, but I can't spend another day with you. Joan."

What happened? Rick was "deaf," and Joan didn't speak loudly enough. By this I mean that Rick was involved in his own life of work, sports, and friends. He thought he was a good "family man." Even though Joan tried to talk about her dissatisfaction, she couldn't make herself heard or understood. And no wonder! Whenever she felt bad, she would smile and talk in quiet, gentle tones. You had to be very perceptive to understand that she was hurting. She didn't look that way or sound that way.

The separation and subsequent divorce were such a blow to Rick that he was determined to be a different person. This time he really would be a good family man. He remarried and became a good stepfather to a four-year-old boy. But what he wanted more than anything else was to show his daughters, who lived with their mother, what a good dad he really was.

Rick didn't realize how inappropriate his behavior was when the girls visited. Every visit was a gala event. Special meals, special events, trips, treats, and presents all marked the occasion. What is more, while the girls were visiting, they could do nothing wrong. He excused the most discourteous, obnoxious behavior imaginable. It got to the point that Barbara, his wife, the non-custodial stepmother, looked for excuses not to be around. Finally, she told Rick that on the weekends when his children were visiting, he should not expect her or her son to be around. They would visit her mother until his children were gone.

By the time Barbara and Rick sought counseling, the marriage was in shambles. Barbara couldn't understand how Rick could expose her to the kind of treatment she got from him and his children every other weekend. Rick couldn't understand why she didn't cooperate with his effort to be a good parent to his children. "After all," he said, "I hardly see them."

Barbara retorted, "And when you do, stop the world; I want to get off!"

"What do you mean by that?"

"I mean that it's unreal. You're not a normal father with

normal kids. You're great with my son. But whenever your girls visit, you do whatever they want. And they do whatever they want without a word of direction or reprimand!''

What was the problem here? Rick had been so shattered by his previous family experience that he was determined to live down his "bad father" name that his former wife had hung on him. He'd show his kids what a great father he was!

The noncustodial father who needs to show what a great father he is really doesn't have his children's best interest at heart. He has his own interest at heart—to show what a great guy he is. This does not help the children. Whether the children are with the custodial parent or the noncustodial parent, they need to understand what the house rules are and what is expected of them. Family life is most enjoyable when the parents are open and available to the children and the children are under control.

The Custodial Child and the Noncustodial Stepparent and Stepsiblings. The child who visits the noncustodial parent must also contend with the noncustodial stepparent and, sometimes, stepsiblings. Gets a bit complicated, doesn't it? Some wisdom needs to be applied here.

Let's go back to Eddie in chapter 1. When Eddie visits his father (the noncustodial parent) for a weekend, he not only must get along with him but also with his noncustodial stepmother, Nancy, and her two daughters, as well as his own sister who lives with them. Eddie is sixteen and the stepsisters are eight and nine. Even though Nancy is his father's new wife and the girls are his father's stepdaughters, this doesn't mean that Eddie has any interest in them. His primary interest is in his father. The others are just part of the package deal.

The reason I point this out is that the noncustodial family should not take offense if Eddie is less than enthusiastic about being with them. As far as he is concerned, they are *his father's* new wife and stepdaughters. Certainly, Eddie should be expected to show courtesy to them, but they should be careful about pushing him into "their" family.

Often, noncustodial families are offended by what appears to be rejection by a visiting child. Put yourself in the child's shoes and you'll understand that it's not a matter of rejection. It's really a matter of neutrality. He had nothing to do with his father's choice of a family or the fact that his father is the noncustodial parent. He may be happy for his father if his father is happy. He should be courteous to "his father's family," but he doesn't have to like them—nor expect them to like him. Perhaps that will come in time if his feelings are respected.

The Need for the Noncustodial Parents

Even though more and more fathers are gaining custody of their children, mother is generally the custodial parent. Though the majority of fathers and children continue to see each other fairly often, after five years three-quarters of these relationships fail to meet the needs of the growing child.[5]

A nine-year-old girl, asked by her mother to write down her feelings about her absent father, wrote this:

Sometimes I feel confused. I have two fathers. One of them lives with me. But the other one lives in Texes. I don't get to see the one who lives in Texes at all. I feel hate and love for him but I don't know how to show it. I don't hear from him at all seen I was 3 years old. And I feel like he dosen't care. But just for once I would like to reach out and love him. But how can I do it, if I do not feel he wants me. I feel sad and sometimes I feel like cring. I have one stepbrother and sister. I get to see them once in a while. But it is better than never.[6]

After reading what her daughter wrote, the mother had this to say:

I must admit that I was very pleased by the lack of attention my daughter received from her biological father, especially after I remarried. It seemed the ideal situation. There was no visitation, no hassles, and eventually no child support, which seemed a reasonable price to pay for his staying out of the way. However, I have come to realize that his total absence may have had more influence on all our relationships than if he had shown interest in his daughter. Coping with the fact that she feels totally rejected by him is a big job for someone so young. In some ways she feels like a part of her is missing. Although she has a tremendous relationship with her stepfather and has asked him to adopt her, he can never replace her biological father. At the same time her biological father could never take the place of her stepdad, who has shared so much in her grow-

ing up. I now am able to see both roles as separate entities. What made the beginning of my marriage so much easier, now causes my daughter a great deal of pain.[7]

Noncustodial mothers and fathers should both maintain contact with their children, even if they are too far away to visit regularly. You don't have to be a superparent. Just let your children know that you are there and that you love them, and do so on a regular basis.

Visitation Dos and Don'ts. Peter Rowlands in *Saturday Parent* offers some helpful dos and don'ts on visiting:

- *Don't* argue with what the other parent may have told the child.
- *Don't* try to cut down the child's positive image of the other parent.
- *Don't* try to persuade your child that you are always right and the other parent is wrong.
- *Don't* react defensively when your child brings home stories about what the other parent is saying about you.
- *Don't* attempt to get the child to offend the religious, moral, or social values of the other family.
- *Don't* use the child as a pawn in a power struggle with the other parent.
- *Do* listen to what your child is saying, and take a friendly interest in him.
- *Do* answer questions in a way that minimizes conflict. You can set rules without being testy about it.
- *Do* be aware of any problems the child may have and what you can do about them.
- *Do* be available on a dependable, reliable basis.
- *Do* show that you have standards of behavior, and even though they may be different from those of the other parent, at least you are consistent.
- *Do* make the visit enjoyable rather than looking at it as a time to impress or persuade the child.[8]

Contacts Other Than Visits. If the noncustodial parent does not live close enough to the child to visit regularly, he or she can keep in touch other ways. Greeting cards on appropriate occasions, such as birthdays and holidays, are a caring gesture.

Letters are always in order. They don't have to be long.

I am not a child of divorce, but I will always remember a letter I received from an uncle when I was about thirteen years old. He knew I was interested in military aircraft, and the year was 1943, the middle of World War II. It was about this time that the first B-29s were coming into production. His letter was about this exciting new bomber, and he drew a diagram of it. I was thrilled that he thought enough about me and my interests to take the time to write to me about something as important as this. I didn't know him very well and rarely saw him. But he cared enough to write me an interesting and exciting letter.

The advent of the cassette tape makes it easy to correspond by tape. Hearing the parent's voice adds an element of intimacy which is absent in a letter.

Finally, use the phone. After-hours rates are quite reasonable. Why not set a regular day and time to call? Five minutes, once a week, from anywhere in the world is little enough to spend on your child to let him know you care and want to be a regular part of his life. He may begin to take this for granted after a while. But being taken for granted is part of being a parent.

In fairness to the custodial parent I should say that these contacts should be monitored. I don't mean censoring or reading letters or listening in to phone conversations. What I mean is that the custodial parent has a responsibility to the child, and to the noncustodial parent, to speak up when the contact becomes problematic for any reason. Parents in the natural family keep each other apprised. The custodial parent should do this for the noncustodial parent as well.

In-laws and Out-laws

Eddie, the stepson in chapter 1, has a large cast of characters to contend with. The chart on page 11 names only part of the cast. If Frank and Nancy (Frank's new wife) have parents who are living, and if Frank's ex-wife's husband's parents are living, it is entirely possible that the cast of seven may actually be thirteen. In one way or another, Eddie could have seven grandparents remotely or directly influencing his life.

Grandparents and Grandchildren. One of the difficulties divorce and remarriage create is the separation of grandparents and grandchildren. Leta felt this keenly when her son Hank and daughter-in-law, Beth, divorced. The three grandchildren, whom she dearly loved, no longer came for visits. Beth not only wrote off the children's father, but also the paternal grandparents.

Leta was angry and hurt. "Beth has no right to do this," she said. "I didn't do anything to her or the children. Just because she's the custodial parent, does this give her the right to cut me off? Does this mean that I am not a noncustodial grandparent, if there is such a thing? I'm going to give Beth a piece of my mind!"

I managed to get Leta settled down and help her see that it wouldn't do a bit of good. She would only add to the tension and estrangement. I suggested that she write her daughter-in-law a letter that went something like this:

Dear Beth,

I'm writing to let you know that I can understand the heartache you've gone through with Hank and to let you know that no matter what has happened between the two of you, I love you and the children. You probably will feel that things aren't the same with us any more. Now I'm "on the other side," one of the "out-laws." But please believe me when I say that what happened is between you and Hank. And I want to leave it there.

Somehow, I'd like to see the grandchildren from time to time. Do you think we could work out some way for this to be done? Please let me hear from you.

Beth did write back, and the two of them worked out a way for grandma to see the grandchildren. What made it work was Leta's determination to let Beth and Hank's divorce be *their* business.

The January 1982 issue of *Stepparent News* carried a "Grandparent Adjustment Survey." This is a result of a survey of family therapists who are members of the American Association for Marriage and Family Therapy. Here are some of the items I have selected from the seventeen listed:

1. Be sensitive to the feelings of all concerned when it comes to the question of whom to invite to family functions.

2. Accept the grandchild's loyalty to the missing parent.

3. Avoid giving unsolicited advice.

4. Be open about your fear of losing the grandchildren.

5. Be prepared to make adjustments in the areas of estate planning, baby-sitting, family get-togethers, and gift giving. Write *Stepparent News* for the complete list.[9]

Everybody's a Family Therapist. It is not likely that all seven grandparents in Eddie's life would have the same interest in him. But it is likely that there would be a lot of talk over two divorces, two remarriages, and four children and stepchildren. Not only would the seven grandparents have their opinions, but so would assorted aunts, uncles, and cousins—much of it within earshot of Eddie. Not only would that be damaging to Eddie (when it is negative and disparaging), but bad advice can be damaging if followed. It seems that everyone's a family therapist!

Pop-psychology books and magazine articles have in recent years produced a more educated public. But a little knowledge can be dangerous. When a family begins to dispense advice, they need to be careful that they are not biased and that they have all the facts and thoroughly understand the family system. More often than not the family is biased and does not fully understand the dynamics of the case.

For example, consider Joan and Rick's situation. Joan spoke bitterly about Rick's insensitivity. "He never listened to me or saw that I was hurting." When I talked to Rick, I realized that he did tend to be self-centered and insensitive. Joan never got his attention until the day she walked out. Whenever she talked about her bad feelings, she covered them with a smile and a sweet voice. Both Joan and Rick were to blame for the breakup. Rick was "deaf" and Joan didn't speak loudly enough!

Family, be careful. Don't be too quick with condemnation or advice. Be warm and supportive, but don't take sides. If you want to help, encourage counseling by either your pastor or a family therapist whom he may recommend.

The Church and the Stepfamily

Not only is the extended family often dragged into stepfamily conflicts; the local church sometimes becomes involved too.

Ken and Sharon's Story. Prior to his marriage to Sharon, Ken was married to Maria. They attended an evangelical church and worked in it for a number of years until their divorce.

The church was rocked by their separation, because it took a very strong stand against divorce, and remarriage was unthinkable. When Maria divorced, she left the church and remarried. The consensus of the congregation was that she had sinned and was out of fellowship with the Lord.

Ken enjoyed a lot of sympathy, as did his daughter, Debbie. In the church's eyes they were the victims of Maria's treachery.

After a few years Ken fell in love with Sharon, whom he had met at church. It wasn't long before he gave her a ring. But their romance created a stir in the church and then a division. Some people sided with the pastor, who felt that Maria's divorce and remarriage was adulterous; therefore, Ken was free to remarry. Others—a much smaller faction—felt that Ken was blameless in the matter of the divorce, but he had no right to remarry. If he did, it would be adultery.

It was only a matter of time until Ken and Sharon married. They decided to marry at home. They did not ask their pastor to officiate, however, because they wanted to avoid conflict with their church.

Things were fairly quiet for a while. Ken and Sharon settled down with Debbie and returned to their usual routine at church. A few members were cool to Ken and Sharon, but most were accepting. All accepted Debbie, and some went even further. Several couples felt that the child was the victim of divorce and subject to a poor testimony of an ''adulterous'' father and stepmother.

It wasn't long before the usual stepparent/stepchild problems started between Sharon and Debbie. And Debbie made the most of it. She began to tell sympathetic people at the church that Sharon didn't want her. She concocted the wildest Cinderella wicked stepmother stories imaginable.

This created a new uproar in the church, already sensitive to the divorce and remarriage of Ken and Sharon. Debbie enjoyed so much attention and sympathy that she told even more incredible tales.

Finally Sharon had had enough. She told Ken that she could not live with the lies and treachery. People at the church were starting to talk about her and would not believe her innocence. "They already want to condemn me for marrying you, Ken. Now I'm the wicked stepmother!"

Ken attempted to solve the problem by sending Debbie to live with her grandmother until he could get the problem under control. But to Debbie's supporters in the church that was the final evidence of Ken's apostasy! Not only had he "disobeyed God"—now he was guilty of "rejecting his own flesh and blood"!

Finally Ken and Sahron left their church and effectively solved their family problem. Debbie lived with her grandmother until she went off to college, while Ken and Sharon settled into a happy life together. But they are drifting from church to church. Ken told me, "We were really burned. Our pastor did everything he could, and I don't blame him a bit. But the people—" Ken paused. "I'm afraid we'll run into the same kind of people wherever we go."

How the Local Church Can Help. The local church has the same impact on Christians as does an extended family. How the brothers and sisters feel about the stepfamily will, to a large extent, facilitate or complicate successful family life for the stepfamily. The church can do three things to assist the stepfamily: exercise understanding compassion, publish a policy statement on divorce and remarriage; and make stepparent education part of their curriculum in family education.

1. *Understanding compassion.* I suggest first of all understanding compassion. I use the adjective "understanding" because compassion toward those suffering the heartaches of divorce and stepfamily adjustment is not a mindless compassion. It is difficult to be compassionate about a problem you don't understand. Conversely, because you do understand, your compassion is believable.

It also is a compassion that is true to your own values. You may believe that divorce and remarriage are totally wrong, and therefore the stepfamily is cursed, disapproved of by God. But this doesn't mean that you are unaccepting. Nonpossessive

128

warmth is applied here. You don't have to agree with the person's choices or lifestyle to be warm and caring. This is what distinguished Jesus' ministry. The woman at the well, the woman caught in adultery, and the tax collectors and sinners He broke bread with all felt His caring.

Divorce, remarriage, and the stepfamilies that are produced as a result are a reality. It is not going to help them to say, "You shouldn't have." The fact is, they have, right or wrong, for good or for bad. Can you minister to their needs while being true to your own convictions and without making them feel condemned? This is *mature* Christianity.

This was the tragedy with Ken, Sharon, and Debbie. Debbie's lies were believed, and her treachery was aided and abetted by a small clique of immature people whose attitude was, "Of course you're suffering, Debbie. You're a *step*child."

2. *Policy statement.* A second thing the local church can do is publish a policy statement on divorce and remarriage. Such a statement should include the following:

a. Does the pastor of the church remarry divorced persons? If so, under what circumstances?

b. Does the church accept into membership persons who have been divorced and remarried? If so, under what circumstances? Does it receive persons who have been divorced and not remarried?

c. Does the church restrict divorced persons or divorced-and-remarried persons from any positions of service or leadership? If so, what are those positions and under what circumstances are those restrictions imposed?

I suggest that the church add to this policy statement anything else that helps clarify their position on divorce and remarriage.

I am not so naive as to believe that merely publishing such a policy statement will solve all the church's problems with divorce, remarriage, and stepfamilies. Some members will privately disagree with it and may fight its implementation. The benefit of the policy statement is that it makes clear to divorced and remarried people what the church's official position is. And when problems do surface in the implementation of the policy, dissenters can be reminded where the church stands. It also gives the leadership of the church a sound basis on which to discipline dissent and schism over this issue in the church.

3. *Education.* Many local churches are doing an excellent job of family education. More and more churches are adjusting to the social reality that single people need to be ministered to. They include the never-married, the widowed, and the divorced. With the rapid increase of stepfamilies, it is essential that the church face this reality too in its educational program.

The philosophy of the educational program for stepfamilies may be stated this way: "This educational program in step-parenting makes no statement of approval or disapproval of divorce or remarriage. If you are remarried and are a stepparent, it is our wish that you be the very best stepparent that you can be. This program is designed for this purpose alone."

The local church has a tremendous opportunity to reach out to stepfamilies with its educational program. Not only can such a program help stepfamilies live together more successfully, it may mean the revitalization of Christian lives and the salvation of the lost.

11.

Evaluating Your Stepfamily System

Now that you have read the theory of successful stepparenting and how you can survive as a stepparent, how does your stepfamily measure up? How would you evaluate its strengths and weaknesses and your strengths and weaknesses as a stepparent or parent in a stepfamily?

Do It Yourself

I have attempted to provide in this book material that will help you to make your own evaluation. Even if you must get help from a family therapist, you will be able to facilitate his work because you are an educated consumer. You should be able to start therapy with a fairly good idea of your stepfamily's strengths and weaknesses. And if you are not yet married but plan to marry someone with children, you should be able to benefit immensely from premarital counseling.

I have already provided some tools for evaluation. One is the Stepparent Test in chapter 2 and the references to it throughout the book. I also have given you some lists of dos and don'ts on pages 97–99, 123.

Understanding Your Family As a System. Let me offer one more aid. Draw a picture of your stepfamily system. It may be simple or complex. The following picture is an example:[1]

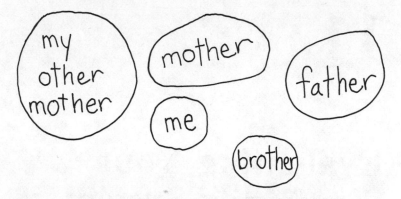

This picture was drawn by a stepson living with his natural father, stepmother, and brother. His natural mother, whom he calls "my other mother," is the largest circle in the picture. She lives many miles away, and he rarely sees her. Occasionally he receives a Christmas or birthday card, but he rarely responds to her.

The important thing is that he responds *internally*. He verbalizes that he is afraid of his "other mother," and when he does hear from her, his emotions are translated into somatic problems such as a stomach ache or diarrhea.

By understanding that the "other mother" looms large in the child's life, the stepmother and father are in a better position to help the boy cope with his fears. They are presented with the delicate task of helping the boy overcome his fears while at the same time not eliminating his mother from the picture.

It is important to understand that the stepfamily is a *system,* not simply the sum of its parts. As a system the members interact and react to each other. And each reaction creates a further reaction.

Think for a moment of the central heating system in your home. Perhaps you have an oil-fired furnace. You have a furnace that burns fuel and blows heat, dampers that regulate the heat flow into the house, and a thermostat that determines how much heat is demanded.

Now let's translate these components into people. "T" (for thermostat) likes the room very warm—eighty degrees. But "D 1, 2, and 3" (dampers) don't like it that hot so they close partially to keep the heat from getting through. This makes "F" (furnace) start heating again to accommodate the thermostat setting. The furnace must work harder than it normally should because it is trying to overcome the resistance of the partially closed dampers. But the dampers still find it too hot, so they close further. The furnace comes on again to accommodate the thermostat.

In this system a lot of unnecessary energy is being burned, and a lot of unnecessary heat is being generated because the dampers and furnace are fighting each other. The thermostat innocently stands by doing nothing, but is in reality the culprit in the battle between the furnace and the dampers. Rather than focus on the furnace and dampers, you should convince the thermostat that sixty-eight degrees (or less) is better than eighty. The result will be less conflict between furnace and dampers and less heat.

How to Draw Your System. Now let's get back to the exercise. Draw a picture of your family system. Be sure to use a large piece of paper so you can fit everyone in.

First, draw a circle of yourself, making it as large or as small as you feel you are in relation to the other people in the system. Label that circle. Now draw a circle for the person in your family to whom you feel closest. Make it as large or small as you feel that person is in relation to yourself. Label that circle.

Second, draw lines of communication between the two circles. If it is good communication, draw a solid line with an arrow indicating direction of flow, such as ——▶. If the flow goes in both directions, it would look like this: ◀——▶.

So far your diagram would look something like this:

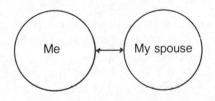

The lines of communication with others in the system may not be as good, however. This will be indicated with a dashed line in the direction of flow, such as --------→ or ◄--------→. No communication would be indicated with an arrow with no connecting line:

Now take a look at your diagram and consider these statements:

1. If the person you feel closest to is your former spouse, it could indicate a problem.

2. If you are an adult in a stepfamily and the person you feel closest to is your mother or father, there could be a problem.

3. If you feel close to no one, there could be a problem.

4. If there is no verbal communication between you and the others in the system, you most assuredly have a problem.

Now add to the diagram the rest of the people in your family system. Connect these people with lines of communication or indicate the lack of them. Here is an example:

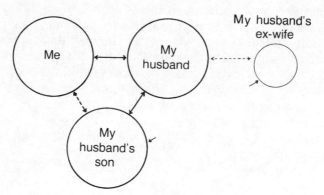

The woman who drew this diagram interprets it this way: "I feel that my husband, stepchild, and I as a family are fairly close. I feel we all are about the 'same size'—of equal importance in the system. My husband and I and he and his son have good communication. The communication between my stepson and myself is poor. My husband's ex-wife is geographically and emotionally very far from us and is small or insignificant. Communication between my husband and his ex-wife is poor, and communication

134 _____

is virtually nonexistent between my stepson and his mother."

The next question is, "What do you want to do about it?" This is tough. As with the heating system, you may have to alter one part of the system to bring the rest of it into balance. This requires that you understand the subtle interactions and reactions in the system. Each of you in the system must be open and communicative about how you feel. Change can come only when there is total awareness and a willingness to change.

In the system diagrammed above, the husband was the key. He had a managerial personality—a take-charge type. He was also guilt-ridden. He felt guilty about his divorce and guilty every time his wife and stepson had the mildest disagreement. He coped with his guilt over the divorce by trying to forget his former wife and get away from her geographically and emotionally as far as he could. His communication with her was poor simply because he didn't want to communicate. He did so only when he had to. His son followed his example and didn't communicate at all for fear of offending his father.

The natural mother felt rejected by both of them, but simply accepted it and didn't try to communicate with either.

The communication between stepmother and stepson was poor because they got the distinct message from father that they could not have any kind of disagreement. If they did, he would take charge of the conversation. And even if they didn't have words, father—who made it a point to be around the house a lot—watched them like a hawk to be sure there "wouldn't be any trouble." The effect was inhibited communication between the stepmother and stepson.

When I showed the father his wife's diagram, he agreed that it was accurate. Improving communication in this stepfamily wasn't so much a matter of getting stepmother, stepson, and former wife to try harder. It was a matter of getting father to back off and let them try!

Choosing a Family Therapist for the Stepfamily

You may discover after drawing your diagrams and discussing them that you are unable to change the system by yourself.

Sometimes it takes someone outside the system to help you understand what is going wrong and to help "the thermostat" see that accepting a sixty-eight-degree setting may be the best solution. "Thermostat" may not think that sixty-eight degrees is "the way it ought to be." But ideas of "oughtness" can be changed.

The May 1981 issue of *Stepparent News* carried a feature on the subject of picking a family therapist. The article urges you to take an active role in the selection of a therapist. He or she should be an expert in stepfamily therapy and knowledgeble about visitation, child support, attorneys, courts, family system dynamics, and grief. You should remember that therapy is not passive. A good therapist doesn't do "it" to the client. He is your hired consultant.

You as a consumer of a service also have a right to know what you are "buying" in terms of service. You should feel free to call the therapist's office and talk about it. Either the therapist or the receptionist should be able to answer your questions. Expect your questions to be answered directly and politely. Remember, you are the consumer of the service. You have a right to know what you're buying. If the therapist is too busy to answer your questions, then he or she is too busy. Find a competent therapist who is not too busy to talk to you. Don't try to get free consultation over the phone, however. Here are some questions you will want answered:

1. Evangelical Christians will want to know if the therapist is a born-again Christian. If not, will he or she respect your Christian convictions?

2. Ask what kind of training and experience he or she has had in family therapy, especially working with stepfamilies.

3. Are his or her services covered under your health care plan?

4. What are the fees and how are they paid? (Usually they are paid when the services are rendered.)

5. How long are the sessions and how frequently does the therapist see his or her clients?

You will find that your phone interview will help you make up your mind. It should take less than five minutes. Again, the purpose of the call is not to get free advice. It is to get information about the therapist.

You can receive more guidance in choosing a stepfamily therapist from the American Association for Marriage and Family Therapy (AAMFT). At your request they will send you their booklet. "What You Should Know About Marriage and Family Therapy," You can obtain the booklet by writing AAMFT, 924 West Ninth St., Upland, CA 91786. Or, you may call their toll-free number. Outside of California it is 800/854-9876. In California call 714/981-0888.

Professional therapists include, but are not limited to, psychologists (Ph.D), clinical social workers (ACSW or MSW), marriage and family therapists (M.A. or Ph.D.), and psychiatrists (M.D.). They have spent six to eight years or more in college and graduate school to earn their advanced degrees. Members of the AAMFT have spent an additional two years as interns, doing therapy under direct supervision.

Degrees and certification are important to the consumer, but don't make these the only criteria. Some impressive-sounding, professional organizations or certification programs simply require attendance of a certification program, lasting from a couple days to much longer, and payment of the program fee. Surprisingly, a few only require yearly dues. The therapist should be able to listen empathetically to your problems. He or she should be able to relate to you as a warm, genuine human being. On the other hand, a willing listener may not have the professional skill to assist, diagnose, or be objective. A blend of academia and empathy is essential.

Cost of therapy varies with the time involved. Therapists charge by the session, usually forty-five to fifty-five minutes. Those in private practice charge between thirty and seventy-five dollars an hour. It used to be that social service agencies, mental health centers, and family service agencies charged according to the client's ability to pay. But shrinking federal and state budgets have forced many social service agencies to charge a full fee, often more than is charged by a therapist in private practice. Don't assume those in private practice charge more than a non-profit agency.[2]

After you have found a therapist, you are not necessarily "locked in." If after one or more visits you decide that you are not happy with his or her services, feel free to say so, terminate, and find someone else. Remember, you are the consumer of the service. You are paying for it, and you have a right to terminate if you are not satisfied. But do the therapist the courtesy of paying for his or her time. And if you do not plan to continue therapy, do the therapist the courtesy of canceling your appointment at least twenty-four hours in advance.

You want to be sure that the reason for your not continuing with the therapist really has to do with your dissatisfaction with service. Some people who seek therapy make it a habit of going from therapist to therapist, changing every time the therapist begins to get at the root of the problem. This type of person is able to give family and friends the appearance of seeking help but effectively avoiding it at the same time.

Talk to Your Pastor. The Christian stepfamily will want to go further, however. One of the major concerns I already have mentioned is the spiritual side of the matter. Is the therapist a born-again Christian or, if not, will he or she understand and respect your Christian convictions rather than seeing Christainity as a neurosis or as the root of problem?

Your pastor will have had some experience in making referrals. He should know what therapists in your area are doing a good job with families and are themselves Christians, or, if they are not, which respect the Christian convictions of the client.

This is also a good way to find a therapist for a family member who lives in another city. Find the name of the best-known evangelical church in the area, and call the church for a name they can recommend. If you don't know how to determine which churches are sound, call a Bible school or seminary that you have confidence in and see if any of their alumni have churches in the city you are trying to contact. Then call that alumnus and find out who the Christian community in his city uses for family therapy.

More About the AAMFT. I want to urge other Christian professionals to become part of the AAMFT. This is the leading clinical professional organization in the field of marriage and family therapy. For nearly forty years the AAMFT has advanced the profession and is now almost ten thousand strong in North America. The basic objectives of the organization are—

- To establish high professional standards of clinical practice;
- To set standards of education and training for professional therapists;
- To establish programs of continuing education and training for professionals;
- To maintain a strict code of professional ethics;
- To cooperate with other helping professionals in the public interest;
- To increase public awareness of the aims and objectives of marriage and family therapy.[3]

Jesus tells us that we are "the salt of the earth." Salt as a preservative is of no value unless it is part of the food to be preserved. Get involved! This is our cultural mandate (Gen. 1:28).

Notes

Preface

1. Brenda Maddox, *The Half-Parent: Living With Other People's Children* (New York: M. Evans, 1975): quoted in *Remarry-O-Gram* 8, no. 1 (Spring 1981): 6. *Remarry-O-Gram* is published by Remarrieds Inc., Box 742, Santa Ana, CA 92701.

Chapter 1

1. Ruth Roosevelt and Jeannette Lofas, *Living in Step* (New York: Stein and Day, 1976), p. 19.
2. Virginia Satir in *Human Behavior* (April 1979): 64.
3. *Stepparent News* 2, no. 6 (October 1981): 2.
4. Anne Lorimer with P. M. Feldman, *Remarriage* (Philadelphia: Running Press, 1980): excerpted in *Remarry-O-Gram* 8, no. 1 (Spring 1981): 3.
5. *Stepparent News* 2, no. 3 (June 1981): 2.
6. Elizabeth Einstein in *Human Behavior* (April 1979): 62–68.
7. Ibid., p. 65.
8. Frank Halse, Jr.: quoted by Elizabeth Einstein in *Human Behavior* (April 1979): 65.

Chapter 2

1. André Bustanoby with Fay Bustanoby, *Just Talk to Me* (Grand Rapids: Zondervan, 1981).
2. Ibid.

Chapter 4

1. *Newsweek* (February 11, 1980).
2. *Stepparent News* 1, no. 6 (October 1980): 3.

3. *Psychology Today* (February 1978): 79.
4. Robert Cassidy, *What Every Man Should Know About Divorce* (Washington, D.C.: Republican Book Publication, n. d.): excerpted in *Stepparent News* 1, no. 9 (January 1981): 3.
5. André Bustanoby, *But I Didn't Want a Divorce* (Grand Rapids: Zondervan, 1977).

Chapter 5

1. *Remarry-O-Gram* 8, no. 1 (Spring 1981): 7.
2. Joseph Goldstein, Anna Freud, and Albert J. Solnit, *Beyond the Best Interests of the Child* (New York: Free Press, 1980): quoted in Roosevelt and Lofas, *Living in Step,* p. 166.
3. Jean Rosenbaum and Veryl Rosenbaum, *Stepparenting* (Corte Madera, Calif.: Chandler and Sharp Publishers, 1977), pp. 37–39.
4. Ibid., p. 40.

Chapter 6

1. Carl R. Rogers, "The Characteristics of a Helping Relationship": quoted in the *Intra-family Communication Training Parent's Manual* (Simi, Calif.; I.C.T. Corp., n.d.): 4.10–4.15.
2. Ibid., 4.13.
3. Ibid.

Chapter 7

1. Roosevelt and Lofas, *Living in Step,* pp. 59–76.
2. *Yours, Mine & Ours: Tips for Stepparents* (Washington, D.C.: U.S. Dept. of Health, Education and Welfare, DHEW Pub. No. [ADM] 78–676, 1978): 15.
3. *Stepparent News* 1, no. 4 (July/August 1980): 3.
4. *Remarry-O-Gram* 8, no. 1 (Spring 1981): 8.

Chapter 8

1. Curt Gallenkamp, "Psychologist Gives Pointers to Stepfathers-to-Be," in *Stepparent News,* 1, no. 3 (June 1980): 2.
2. Roosevelt and Lofas, *Living in Step,* p. 81.
3. See Venita Van Caspel, *Money Dynamics: How to Build Financial Independence* (Reston, Va.: Reston Publishing, n.d.), 37 pp.
4. Roosevelt and Lofas, *Living in Step,* p. 95.
5. *Marriage and Divorce Today* 7, no. 17 (November 30, 1981): 2.
6. Ibid., no. 20 (November 30, 1981): 4.
7. Ibid., no. 8 (November 30, 1981): 3.
8. Judith Herman and Lisa Hirschman in *Marriage and Divorce Today* 7, no. 8 (September 28, 1981): 3–4.

Chapter 9

1. *People* (November 16, 1981): 104.
2. *Stepparent News* 2, no. 2 (June 1981): 3.
3. *People* (November 16, 1981): 105.
4. Roosevelt and Lofas, *Living in Step,* pp. 153–55.
5. A subscription to *Stepparent News* costs $9 per year for individuals as of September 1982. Write 8716 Pine Street, Gary, IN 46403.

Chapter 10

1. *Stepparent News* 1, no. 2 (May 1980): 3.
2. "The C E U Clearing House," published by The Maryland Foundation, Adelphi, Md. (Winter 1982), p. 10.
3. A group you may want to learn more about is Solo Ministries, Inc., 8740 East 11th Street, Suite Q, Tulsa, OK 74112. You may want to subscribe to their magazine, called *Solo,* a Christian magazine for single adults. The organization sponsors singles conferences.
4. "The C E U Clearing House," p. 10.
5. *Psychology Today* (January 1980): 67.
6. *Stepparent News* 1, no. 1 (April 1980): 3.
7. Ibid.
8. *Stepparent News* 2, no. 7 (November 1981): 1.
9. See chapter 9, footnote 6, for the address of *Stepparent News.*

Chapter 11

1. Adapted from *Stepparent News* (January–May 1981).
2. *Stepparent News* 2, no. 2 (May 1981): 1–2.
3. "What You Should Know About Marital and Family Therapy" (Upland, Calif.: American Association for Marriage and Family Therapy, n.d.).

Index